GOLDEN HART GUIDES

TRADITIONAL BRITAIN

GOLDEN HART GUIDES

Traditional Britain

Mark Martin

SIDGWICK & JACKSON LONDON
in association with Trusthouse Forte

Contents

Front cover photo: Hastings town crier
Back cover photo: Up-Helly-A, Lerwick
Frontispiece: Changing the Guard,
Buckingham Palace

Photographs by the British Tourist
Authority, with the exception of
p 25 (Barnaby's Picture Library);
26 (Camera Press); 48 (Ottery News)
Line drawings by Paul Watkins

Compiled and designed by Paul Watkins
Editorial assistant: Sarah Jane Evans

First published in Great Britain 1983
by Sidgwick & Jackson in association
with Trusthouse Forte

Copyright © 1983 Mark Martin

ISBN 0-283-98913-0

Photoset by Robcroft Ltd, London WC1
Printed and bound in Great Britain
by Hazell Watson and Viney Limited,
Aylesbury, Bucks
for Sidgwick & Jackson Limited,
1 Tavistock Chambers, Bloomsbury Way,
London WC1A 2SG

Introduction This book deals with British traditions, customs and seasonal events. The opening section goes through the seasons, concentrating on national customs and traditions which take place at certain times of year. Within this section are a variety of traditional British recipes, from haggis to hot punch, which give the seasons their special flavour. The second half of the book is divided into 14 regional sections, which list almost 200 particular events. Each event is described, giving details of where and when it takes place, its origins, and what you can expect to see.

The emphasis of this book is on customs and traditions that are still practised today, and can be seen in something approaching their original setting. With the coming of industrialization and urban growth, much of our heritage of traditional activity has lapsed. There has, however, been a growing awareness of this area of our culture, and in recent years revivals have been staged – in some cases proving more popular than their originals. A notable example is the Welsh Eisteddfod, which has now branched out to include international folk gatherings of world-wide repute and popularity.

The topics covered in this book range from simple village celebrations and local superstitions, to such renowned events as Trooping the Colour and the Edinburgh Festival. Most of the events and traditions mentioned can be seen free, and many include a certain amount of audience participation. Geographically these range from the Helston Furry Dance in Cornwall to the Up-Helly-A celebrations in the Shetlands, and the variety of these activities and their origins reflect the richness of our historical and racial heritage. Many of our village traditions hark back to pre-Christian practices. Druid and Viking rites and Celtic and Anglo-Saxon customs are still present in many areas. Other customs commemorate specific historical events, such as Guy Fawkes Night or Oak Apple Day. Others still are linked to specific places, such as Nottingham Goose Fair, the National Town Crier's Championship at Hastings, or the Relief of Derry celebrations. Wherever you go throughout Britain, at whatever time of year, you'll find that there's usually some traditional event taking place somewhere nearby.

To Everything There is a Season

New Years For Old

In New Guinea there is a primitive tribe which still believes that unless it holds a particular ceremony each morning to bring up the sun the world will remain in darkness. In modern Britain we consider that we have evolved beyond such practices – yet we still believe in 'bringing in' the New Year.

A widespread custom for greeting the New Year is **First Footing**. This is still prevalent throughout Britain, and especially in Scotland where there are several variations. Traditionally, the first person to cross the threshold in the New Year affects the fate of that household throughout the coming year. This First Foot, as he (or she) is called, may be a chance passer-by but is more usually someone who comes on purpose to bring in the New Year.

For good luck the First Foot carries certain symbolic gifts. A crust of bread (or piece of cake) and a lump of coal (or peat) ensure food and warmth. For happiness he brings drink, and for wealth he brings a coin or salt. (This latter gift dates from the time when many people, including the Roman garrisons, were paid in this vital commodity: our word salary deriving from the Latin word *sal*, which means salt.) Possibly owing to a native thriftiness, the giving of a coin seems largely to have lapsed in Scotland. Instead, in the fishing villages of East Fife the First Foot presents a red herring; while in other parts he brings a concoction known as 'Het Pint'. This consists of a mixture of spirits, beer, sugar and egg – perhaps on the assumption that if you can survive this you can survive the coming year!

By tradition, the First Foot is heartily welcomed and greets each member of the family in turn. Though in some parts of Scotland the First Foot must not say a word until he has placed a lump of coal or piece of peat on the hearth – the heart of the household and centre of family life. The First Foot is not allowed to be a member of the family, and he should be young, healthy and good-looking. If he has a limp, is cross-eyed, or his eyebrows join across the top of his nose, these are taken as bad omens. Likewise, he should not be dressed in black – though if he has a dark complexion or dark hair this brings good luck. Red hair is taken as a very bad sign – a belief which almost certainly stems from the days of the Viking raids. In most parts of Britain tradition has it that the First Foot should be male, though in the Isle of Man the 'Quaaltagh', as the First Foot is known, can be either sex. Throughout England and Wales, if the First Foot is a woman that is said to presage disaster.

To this day, in certain Welsh border villages a woman approaching a house on New Year's Day will shout before entering to ask whether the house has been First Footed. To enter without doing so is considered an act of malice (and the person doing so often used to be considered a witch). Formerly, in the West Country and the North of England, First Footing was also practised to bring in Christmas.

The Twelve Days of Christmas

In previous centuries the Twelve Days of Christmas were taken as a holiday in all rural areas. Naturally, the feeding and milking of animals continued; but such onerous tasks as ploughing and hauling ceased. This midwinter break was celebrated all over Europe, and may well derive at least in part from the curious custom of blooding the horses, which was carried out on St Stephen's Day (December 26th). According to popular notion, the blood of working horses became thick and hot when they had to spend too much time idle in their stables because of the weather. To combat this the owners drained the 'bad blood' by making an incision in the jugular vein. The horses then had to be rested for the next ten days. This custom was widespread until well into the last century, and its beneficial effects are not entirely dismissed by modern veterinary science, given the inferior conditions and feeding habits of those days.

The end of this holiday was **Twelfth Night**, traditionally a night of revelry and good cheer before the return to work. Twelfth Night parties are still a regular feature of the Christmas scene throughout the country, and many still include traditional features. Bull masks are worn, fantastic disguises are adopted, and the proceedings are presided over by a King of Misrule, who is elected for the day. In many parts of the country a plum pudding was baked with a bean in it, and pieces of the cake would be distributed throughout the village. The person who found the bean in his slice became the King of Misrule. Only in Victorian times did this custom become attached to Christmas, when a silver coin (usually a threepenny piece) was substituted for the bean. This is a custom which remains widespread – though alterations to the silver coinage have increasingly made it something of a dental hazard.

Another widely observed custom associated with Twelfth Night and the end of the holiday is the taking down of Christmas decorations. If these are left up after January 6th it is said to bring bad luck. In a recent survey, this was found to be one of the most widely held seasonal superstitions throughout the land. Why is this so? And why also do we put up decorations in the first place? Traditionally the Christmas holiday was a time of rejoicing and merriment; but it was also the dark midwinter period when many believed that the spirits of the dead roamed abroad. In Europe werewolves appeared in the woods, in Norway the dreaded trolls came down from the mountains, and in Britain our fairies emerged together with Will-o'-the-Wisp. It appears that in several rural areas Christmas decorations included charms, such as mistletoe and wild garlic, whose purpose was to ward off these evil spirits; and if these charms were left up too long after the holiday they lost their effectiveness. This aptly demonstrates how the echoes of such superstitious folklore die hard, even when we are no longer aware of their significance.

Plough Sunday, Plough Monday

The first Sunday after Twelfth Night is called **Plough Sunday**. This was once as widely observed in the Church calendar as Harvest Sunday, but full Plough Sunday services are now held only in Exeter, Salisbury and Kent. At these, the plough is brought into the church and blessed, before it is tak-

en out to plough the first furrow of the New Year. The actual ploughing takes place on **Plough Monday**, which paradoxically is observed over a much wider area, especially in Devon and Lincolnshire.

On Plough Monday the village lads dress in rosettes and horse ribbons and are roped to a decorated plough. They then drag the plough from door to door accompanied by fiddles, pipes and an accordion. At each door they are given alms, and any reluctant donors are liable to have their front garden ploughed up! In the evening there is usually a celebration in the local pub and the money collected is donated to charity. In some villages it is traditional to bury a 'corn dolly', made from the last stalks of the previous harvest, under the peeled turf of the first furrow ploughed. The main reason why Plough Monday customs died out over much of Britain was because the local lads with their plough often didn't know when to stop – with the result that the villagers frequently had to barricade themselves in their homes to stop being set upon by drunken revellers with blackened faces demanding money. Many elderly rural folk remember to this day their childhood nightmare of seeing these blackened faces at the window.

Plough Monday is sometimes called 'St Distaff's Day'. There is, however, no St Distaff to be found in the records. This was merely the day when the distaff side of the family were meant to go back to work. After the great 'holiday' spent preparing and clearing up after all the festivities this may well have come as something of a relief, with the womenfolk voicing ironic blessings to their 'saint'.

Hatfuls, Capfuls, and Three Bags Full

Wassailing the apple trees is an old West Country custom whose origins may well date from pre-Christian times. The word wassail derives from the Anglo-Saxon *wes hál*, meaning 'be whole' or 'be hail' (in good health). As with many country customs its effects are both practical and cheering. A wassail cup of mulled cider or hot punch is passed from hand to hand. Afterwards, fortified against the cold, the villagers set out into the apple orchards where bonfires are lit.

These have the beneficial effect of protecting the trees from frost. The original custom was part of the old Twelfth Night celebrations, but when the calendar was changed in 1752 the country folk quite rightly refused to believe that Mother Nature would take any notice of such new-fangled notions, so the custom continued to be celebrated on the old Twelfth Night, which is now January 16th.

In parts of Somerset a Wassail Queen is carried shoulder-high through the orchard and pours a libation into the fork of each tree, whilst behind her the farmers discharge volleys of shot through the branches. Some believe the gunshot was intended to drive away evil spirits; but before the invention of guns the custom simply involved making a lot of noise – a great hullabaloo of shouting and banging pots probably intended to wake up the slumbering gods of fertility. After this, the musicians strike up the Wassailing Song, part of which runs:

> Let every man take off his hat and shout to thee,
> Old Apple Tree, Old Apple Tree,
> We wassail thee, and hoping thou wilt bear
> Hat fulls,
> Cap fulls,
> And three bushel bag fulls,
> And a little heap under the stairs.

This custom was once prevalent all over England, especially in the apple orchard counties of Devon, Somerset, Hereford and Kent. Now it survives only in three or four villages in the West Country. The best known celebration is held at Monty's Court, Norton Fitzwarren, near Taunton, the home of Colonel Mitford-Slade, the Lord Lieutenant of Somerset.

Spring and a Young Man's Fancy

An old wives' tale has it that the weather on **St Paul's Day**, January 25th, is an omen of the weather to come throughout the year. This superstition prevails in many parts of the country, and often goes beyond mere weather. Sun is said to betoken a good year, rain or snow a continuation of the common grind, mist brings scarcity, and thunder or high wind presage death or war. On the Isle of Man there's an old Manx saying:

> Wind and storm on St Paul's,
> Great war and much death befalls.
> Sun and fair sky on that day,
> Much corn and good making of hay.

In certain parts of the West Country, especially in Wiltshire and Cornwall, it's a widely held superstition that **Candlemas** (February 2nd) is the day on which the first snowdrops appear – thus demonstrating the somewhat whimsical relation of superstition to reality. Yet the origins of these superstitions are seldom whimsical. Even the Candlemas superstition probably derives from this, being the time when you can start looking for the first signs of spring, together with an association of the white snowdrops with the purification rites of the original Candlemas (when mothers were required to carry candles to church on their first visit after childbirth).

However, there's nothing whimsical about **St Valentine's Day**, which is now the third most popular card-sending occasion in the year (after Christmas and birthdays). Even the 'serious' papers devote columns of small advertisements to such poetic Valentine's Day greetings as 'cuddley-wuddley loves his mopsy-popsy'. According to the ancient tradition of St Valentine's:

> This is the day birds choose their mate
> And I choose you if I'm not too late.

Historically speaking, there were two St Valentines – both churchmen said to have been martyred four years apart on the same day in Italy in the middle of the third century. Various more or less fanciful legends exist concerning the exploits of these two figures, but none is based on a scrap of fact. The customs of St Valentine's Day almost certainly stem from the Roman feast of the Lupercalia – which was in small part a fertility rite, and in large part an excuse for a grand old Roman revel, including the drawing of lots for partners. With the coming of the Christian era, this custom was discreetly dropped, which is perhaps fortunate for the memory of the departed St Valentines.

Nowadays the customs of St Valentine's Day dictate that you send to your love an anonymous message, a gift, billet-doux, or card decorated with a gushing verse and a pink satin heart. According to the Valentine's Day card manufacturers at least 30 per cent of these are sent as jokes, yet the remaining 70 per cent continue to demonstrate the truth of the old adage that when love strikes we are blind!

The Long Days of Lent

The forty days of the Lenten Fast are preceded by **Shrove Tuesday**. In the days when Lent was still strictly observed, this was sometimes known as 'Faster's E'en'. Shrove Tuesday was the day on which people were expected to 'shrive' (confess) their sins before Lent. Otherwise known as 'Guttit Tuesday' or 'Doughnut Day', it's now popularly called 'Pancake Day'. The original idea of eating pancakes was to use up all the meat, butter and eggs which couldn't be eaten in Lent. Once again, this had practical significance. Eggs became plentiful at this time of year, and were a source of great temptation when there wasn't much food around. However, if the eggs were left uneaten they would hatch into chickens at Eastertide. The pancakes themselves probably originate from the small wheatcakes which were eaten at early spring festivals in pre-Christian times, and in Scotland they still eat bannocks, which are made out of oatmeal.

Shrove Tuesday has always involved boisterous celebrations, and all over the country pancake races are held, in which the contestants run with a frying pan, at the same time tossing their pancakes in the air. The best known of these are held at Olney in Buckinghamshire and Lincoln's Inn Fields in London. In several villages in Northumbria and the Midlands, Shrovetide football matches are held. These tend to be wild games with the minimum of rules. At Ashbourne in Derbyshire the game begins at 2 pm and often goes on until midnight. Here the goals are two mills three miles apart, with several muddy streams between

Pancakes

If you want to eat and enjoy pancakes, then don't toss them. Leave that to those who are running the races, and instead savour a paper-thin pancake too fine to be turned without the support of a palette knife.

4oz (125g) plain flour
pinch of salt
1 egg
1 egg yolk
½ pint (30cl) milk
1 tbsp oil
white vegetable fat
sugar and lemons

Sift together the flour and salt. Make a hollow in the centre and add the egg, egg yolk and half the milk. Stir carefully to form a smooth batter. Add the remaining milk and oil.

Put a little fat in a frying pan and heat until smoking hot. Quickly pour in 2 tbsp of batter, tipping the pan to make a thin pancake. Cook over moderate heat until the underside is browned, then turn and cook the other side.

Sprinkle with sugar and lemon juice. Roll up and serve with more lemon.

them, and the teams consist of an unlimited number from the Upper end of the village against those who live in the Down end.

In former centuries Shrove Tuesday was a great cock-fighting day, and until the early decades of this century there was a custom in Brighton that a chicken was hauled above a street in an earthenware pot. People were allowed four shies at the pot, and whoever broke it won the chicken. Like many picturesque customs this has origins in more brutal rites. In this case, 'Thrashing the Hen' – a vicious pastime which needs no description. Yet even this had its arcane significance. Until the last century in certain Cotswold villages hens were traditionally beaten at this time of year if they didn't produce eggs – a quaint way of ritualising an all too natural vexation! The reason why chickens and eggs appear so much associated with customs at this time of year is because the laying and hatching of eggs were all-

important in rural communities, often making the difference between a balanced diet or hunger during the coming year.

On the day after Shrove Tuesday comes **Ash Wednesday**, the first day of Lent. This name probably derives from some pre-Christian ceremony whose origins are forgotten. In Christian times the name became associated with a service where the priest blessed a heap of ashes, often following this ritual with a 'fire and brimstone' sermon in which he reminded his parishioners that one day they too would become ashes. On the first day of Lent, especially in Roman Catholic services in Ireland, the priest marks the foreheads of his parishioners with a dab of burnt cork (which is not washed off until nightfall).

The main relief from the Lenten Fast comes on the fourth Sunday in Lent. This was once called 'Mid-Lent Sunday', but is now better known as **Mothering Sunday**. This was traditionally the day on which every servant and apprentice was granted leave to return to visit his mother. (Though some authorities consider that the 'mother' referred to here was their 'mother church'.) Either way, it was a day of homecoming and the bringing of gifts.

The traditional Mother's Day gifts are posies of violets or primroses and Simnel Cake, which is a spiced fruit cake, often with a layer of almond paste cooked in the middle. For this reason, the day is sometimes known as 'Simnel Sunday'. There are several distinct regional varieties of Simnel Cake, the best known coming from Shrewsbury, Devizes and Bury. The name 'Simnel' comes from *simila*, the Latin word for fine-grained wheat

Simnel Cake

Tradition has it that 12 almond paste balls should be set around the cake representing the 12 apostles. Some reduced the number to 11, to be sure of excluding Judas. Either way, this cake is a delicious interruption to the Lenten fast. Though the religious significance of the fast is often forgotten today, many still use Lent as a light-hearted means of weaning themselves off a particular indulgence: chocolate, puddings, cigarettes, or a favourite drink.

5 oz (150g) butter
4 oz (125g) sugar
2 tsp golden syrup, (warmed)
3 eggs, beaten
8 oz (250g) flour
12 oz (375g) mixed dried fruit
1 oz (30g) candied peel
1/2 tsp mixed spice
1/2 tsp ground cinnamon
1/2 tsp ground cloves
milk
1 lb (500g) almond paste
apricot jam, (warmed)

Cream the butter and sugar. Stir the syrup and eggs into the butter. Mix the dry ingredients together and stir them gradually into the butter mixture. The cake should be fairly stiff, but add a little milk, if necessary.

Put half the mixture into a lined, greased 10in (25cm) cake tin. Roll out half the almond paste to 1/4in (.5cm) thickness and press it down over the cake, making sure there are no bubbles.

Add the remaining cake mixture. Bake in a preheated oven 150°C (300°F or Mark 2) for about 2¼ hrs or until the cake has risen well and is firm to the touch.

When the cake is cold, spread the warm jam over the top and cover it with the remaining almond paste. Alternatively, make a ring of 12 (or 11) balls of almond paste round the rim. Brown the paste lightly under the grill.

---

flour, and the cakes probably date from the Roman occupation. The earliest historical reference to them is by Edward the Confessor.

The traditions of Mothering Sunday had all but died out by the first half of this century, but since the Second World War the day has made a widespread and commerc-ially-encouraged comeback. This is thought to be a legacy from the American servicemen who were billeted over here during the war. They mistook Mothering Sunday for their own Mother's Day, which falls around the same time. In fact, the two do not share any common origins – the American day was in-augurated in 1907 as the result of an almost single-handed campaign by Miss Anna Jarvis of Philadelphia, whose mother had just died.

The other widely-observed break from Lent is **St David's Day**, which falls on March 1st. St David is the patron saint of Wales, and on this day it is a custom amongst ex-iled Welsh preachers to return to their country of origin and deliver fiery sermons. Another custom, which is alas all but extinct, saw Welsh villagers and farming folk rallying round to help anyone who through sickness or misfortune had been unable to plough his land be-fore this date. A traditional gift of leeks was also brought along to fill out the pot, and the helping hands provided jovial company at the end of the day.

No Fooling like Old Fooling

After the long rigours of the winter, **April Fool's Day** comes as a welcome surprise – though less welcome for some than for others. Sometimes known as 'All Fools' Day' or 'April Noddy Day', this celebration has acquired similar customs all over Europe, and even as far afield as India (where they have a Huli Fool's Day at the end of March). Most of the pranks performed on April Fool's Day are sheer schoolboy stuff, with no great premium on originality. However, an elaborate early English example of an April Fool's Day joke was carried out in 1698, when someone sent out a number of invitations to important citizens asking them along to witness the 'Washing of the Lions' in the moat of the Tower of London – a non-event which drew an appreciable crowd. To reinforce the notion that these April Fool's Day surprises have little to do with originality, the same joke was played again in 1860 – apparently with equal success.

In Scotland there's an elaboration called 'sending someone on a Gowk's Errand' (a gowk is a cuckoo). The victim is given a sealed note to take to a house. On the note is written 'Gowk's Errand', and the receiver of the note is expected to send the hapless victim on to another house, where the same thing should happen. This can go on until midday, when all April fooling stops. Should anyone attempt to play a joke after midday the traditional reply is:

> April Fool's is gone and past
> I'm the one who laughs the last.

Whereupon the joker is expected to shrivel with embarrassment at the mockery of the assembled company.

There are many theories as to the origin of April Fool's Day – none is definitive. The fact that this day falls close to the vernal Equinox and that the revels cease at an appointed hour suggest that April Fool's Day may well derive from the Roman feast of the Saturnalia or the subsequent medieval Feast of Fools. At this feast servants could mock their masters, ceremonials were subjected to burlesque, and in general it came to be looked upon as an underdog's day.

Whatever its origins, the observance of April Fool's Day obviously fulfills some perennial need in man's character for licensed japery and the letting-off of steam, and as such the day shows no sign of lapsing, either in the classroom or in the home, or the office, or on the factory floor. Today, even the television news on April 1st is liable to include an April Fool's item – such as the celebrated film report, accompanied by a suitable po-faced commentary, on the Italians gathering in the spaghetti harvest from trees.

A similar, though rather more schoolboy-ish ritual, is observed on the first day of every month in schools throughout the country. This entails creeping up behind someone, giving him or her a sneaky pinch and a punch, and shouting as quickly as possible:

> A pinch and a punch
> for the first of the month!

Should the victim not be as surprised as expected and respond by shouting 'White Rabbits!' before you can finish the rhyme, he or she is then allowed to pinch and punch you. As many a weary schoolteacher knows, these observances are all too liable to degenerate into general mayhem. However, like April Fool's Day jokes, this practice also thankfully ceases at midday.

Easter

The celebration of Easter marks the end of Lent. This is a moveable feast as Easter Day is the first Sunday after the full moon on or after March 21st (though when the full moon actually falls on a Sunday, Easter is the next Sunday). Easter Sunday thus falls between March 22nd and April 25th.

The Sunday preceding Easter is called **Palm Sunday**. Church services on this day involve a solemn procession with the bearing of palm leaves (in England usually willow, dried desert grass or even lilac). This is to mark the entry of Christ into Jerusalem on a donkey, when the crowds strewed palm leaves in his path. Throughout the centuries all kinds of ancient superstitions and spring customs have attached themselves to this ceremony, only to fall into abeyance, so that the church ceremony now remains as it once was – a pious commemoration of an event of no fundamental theological significance which took place at the gates of a provincial city over 4000 miles away on a Sunday nearly 2000 years ago.

The following Thursday is known as **Maundy Thursday**. On this day the Church commemorates Christ commanding his disciples to love one another, and then washing their feet. Until the reign of James II, on this day it was customary for the monarch to wash the feet of as many poor people as there were years in his reign. An echo of this custom survives in the Maundy Service at Westminster Abbey which is attended by the Queen. After the service the Queen distributes specially-minted Maundy Money to as many poor people as there are years in her reign – though nowadays this rare coinage is quickly snapped up by dealers.

Apart from religious observance there are two prevailing customs associated with **Good Friday**. In the West Country this is traditionally the day for planting potatoes and parsley. (Also, in these parts it is considered bad luck to put to sea to fish on this day, or even fish from land.) Much more widespread is the tradition of Hot Cross Buns – though anticipation of this Good Friday event means that these buns now appear for sale almost from the beginning of Lent, thus nullifying the whole significance of the custom. Traditionally Hot Cross Buns are baked from the leftover sacramental bread used for the Good Friday services. The buns are spiced, contain currants, and are marked with a cross – as were the ancient sacramental loaves. The buns should be eaten at breakfast and in former times were sold by wandering vendors, whose street cry is still a popular nursery rhyme:

Hot Cross Buns! Hot Cross Buns!
One a penny, two a penny,
Hot Cross Buns!
If you have no daughters
Give them to your sons.
One a penny, two a penny
Hot Cross Buns!

Hot Cross Buns

Once only eaten (or sold on Good Friday – but the tradition has lapsed.

1 lb (500g) strong plain flour
¼ tsp salt
1 oz (30g) fresh yeast
2 oz (60g) sugar
4 fl oz (12.5cl) milk
4 fl oz (12.5cl) boiling water
3 oz (90g) butter
1 egg, beaten
1 tsp ground cinnamon
1 tsp grated nutmeg
1 tsp mixed spice
½ tsp ground mace
3 oz (90g) raisins
2 oz (60g) chopped peel
2 oz (60g) almond paste or shortcrust pastry
Glaze
beaten egg
2 oz (60g) sugar
5 tbsp water

Put the flour, salt and spices in a bowl. Crumble the yeast into a bowl, and add 1 heaped tsp of the sugar and 4oz (125g) of the flour. Mix together the milk and water and gradually stir into the yeast. Leave for 15 mins to froth up.

Mix the rest of the sugar into the flour and rub in the butter. Add the egg and the yeast mixture, and mix to a dough. Knead for 10 min. Then leave the dough to rise (takes 1-2 hrs).

Break down the risen dough, add the fruit and peel and roll it out into a sausage. Cut into 18 discs and shape them into buns. Roll out the almond paste and cut it into thin strips. Brush the buns with the beaten egg and lay out the strips to form a cross on each bun. Leave to prove for 15 – 30 min, then bake in a preheated oven 230°C (450°F or Mark 8) for 10 – 15 min.

Boil together the water and sugar for 2 – 3 min and brush the glaze over the hot buns when they come out of the oven.

Eat hot with plenty of butter.

According to no less an authority than the Venerable Bede the word **Easter** comes from the Anglo-Saxon word *Eostre*, which was the name of the Goddess of Spring and Dawn. In the Saxon calendar the month of April was known as 'Eosturmonath'.

In bygone centuries countless local rural springtide customs and observances became associated with Easter, and all kinds of weird and wonderful Easter traditions are still prevalent throughout the land. The best known of these are Easter Eggs, or Pace Eggs as they are still sometimes known in the North. (Pace derives from Paschal – as in Paschal Lamb – which itself derives from the Jewish feast of Passover.) Since Victorian times Easter Eggs have often been made of chocolate, marzipan or other types of confectionery. Yet the custom of using genuine hard-boiled eggs still survives in countless households, even those where the religious observances are largely ignored. Traditionally these boiled eggs are dyed and decorated. One of the most popular ways of decorating them is by marking flower shapes on the outer shell with wax and then boiling the egg inside an onion skin – this gives a deep brown colour with little white flower patterns. However, the most traditional colour for dying the eggs is red. This comes from the legend that Our Lady stood below the cross with a basket of eggs, which were splattered with the blood of Christ.

More significantly, Easter Eggs are the traditional symbol of resurrection and re-birth. As such, they are attached to spring ceremonies all over the world well before

Christian times, most notably in China and ancient Egypt. The custom of rolling eggs is also widely observed. Sometimes the eggs are rolled down a hill until they crack, and sometimes they are raced. They can also be marked with lucky and unlucky signs, the one which falls the furthest giving an omen of future luck. These quaint customs originate in pre-Christian rites whose exact significance is now lost in legend, (just as, in Eastern Europe, Easter Eggs are still placed on the graves of the recent dead, or buried in vineyards). Though the custom of rolling eggs is on the decline in this country, it has thrived in America – where large numbers of eggs are traditionally rolled on the lawns of the White House each Easter Monday.

A popular Easter figure is the Easter Hare. According to tradition he is the one who hides the Easter Eggs, and it is still a popular custom to send out the children to hunt for the eggs which have been 'hidden by the Easter Hare' (who sometimes, especially in America, is known as the Easter Rabbit). This too is a pre-Christian custom, dating from Celtic rites, when it was believed that the hare chased away the spirit of winter. This also accounts for the popular tradition of eating hare pie at Easter.

Throughout the regions there are many different Easter customs. The best known of these are the Easter bonnet parades – which originated with the tradition of putting on fresh bright clothes with the coming of Spring (a custom of distinctly refreshing significance in rural areas where the poor yeomen were often sewn into oiled undergarments for the duration of the winter to keep them warm). Other Easter customs include a wide variety of local activities from fairs and cart-horse parades to the famous bottle-kicking match at Hallaton in Leicestershire.

Easter Parade, Battersea Park

Ale and Hearty

St George's Day (April 23rd) is marked throughout England by the flying of the red-crossed flag of St George on church towers. Despite his origins as an obscure martyr in Asia Minor, St George has been the patron saint of England since the 14th century – when he took over from the more likely St Edward (better known as King Edward the Confessor). Until the last century there was a tradition in some areas of serving free ale on St George's Day, a custom which has had a commercially-inspired partial revival at least in London, where a pub chain serves beer at a nominal price on this day. However, in Norwich it is St George's traditional adversary which is remembered. Here the mayor and aldermen march in procession to the cathedral followed by a green and gold dragon known as 'Snap'. During the service the dragon has to sit outside the cathedral on a special 'Dragon's Stone'.

Another quaint custom associated with this time of year is the hearing of the 'first cuckoo'. For a century or so it has been customary for the person who thinks he has heard the first cuckoo of spring to write to *The Times* about it – and most years a 'first cuckoo' letter is still printed. However, customs associated with cuckoos were prevalent throughout the land long before *The Times* appeared – though all of these have since lapsed. The only remaining feature of these customs is linguistic. The word cuckoo is still used to describe a person or behaviour that is considered slightly mad. This originates from Anglo-Saxon times, and was the derisive name used to describe the Celts, whom the Anglo-Saxons considered stupid and unintelligent because they didn't understand Anglo-Saxon.

May Day and All's Well

Since time immemorial **May Day** has been a day of rejoicing. This is the traditional beginning of summer – and is celebrated as such despite the vagaries of the weather. It was only a few years ago that England was covered in a blanket of snow on May Day, thus reinforcing the ancient popular adage:

> Ne'er cast a clout
> Till May is out.

(A clout, in this instance, being an article of clothing.)

The first of May was originally a Quarter Day in the old pagan pastoral calendar. In those days it was called 'Beltane', which means goodly fire. At this time it was customary to set fire to the gorse to drive away any evil sprits or witches. Only after this was it thought to be safe to let the cattle out to graze on the pastures. May Day observances are found all over Europe, many originating from the Roman festival of the Floralia – whose observances, as with so many Roman feasts, appear to have degenerated in later years to orgies.

The central emblem of the May Day rituals is the May Pole. Once upon a time this was certainly a phallic symbol in some ancient fertility rite. In many villages the pole used to be a lopped tree, which was brought into the village under cover of darkness and set up on the green on May Eve. Traditional dancing around the May Pole is still a widespread custom, with garlanded girls weaving patterns into the ribbons attached to the top of the pole. The May Pole is usually painted in spiralling colours, and centuries ago there was one on every village green. In 1661, after the Restoration, a 134ft May Pole was set up in London's Strand, where it stood for half a century. Nowadays the tallest May Pole is over 80ft and stands at Barwick in Elmet near Leeds. In the West Country there used to be a custom of trying to steal May Poles from neighbouring villages, with each village mounting guard on its May Pole throughout May Eve. This custom of mounting guard still persists in Lanreath in Cornwall.

Morris Dancing is another popular tradition attached to May Day. At present this pursuit is undergoing a welcome revival which extends far beyond May Day celebrations. The word 'Morris' comes from 'Moorish', though this form of dancing would appear to have nothing to do with the ancient Moors of North Africa. In times gone by 'Moor' was a term for any foreigner, and the dance was probably imported from Europe with the Normans. Morris dancing remains little changed from the 15th century. The participants are usually six men dressed in knee-breeches, sporting flower-decked hats and bells. They carry staves and are accompanied by an accordion or flute. Nowadays Morris dancers are liable to pop up in the most unlikely places, even appearing in summer outside pubs in the City of London – though the gusto with which they perform their dances, as well as their traditional thirst for ale, remain undiminished.

The most prevalent May Day custom used to be May Birching. On May Day Eve the village lads and maidens would head for the woods to gather sprigs and garlands. This is the traditional time of 'Spring and a young man's fancy . . . ' and not unnaturally mothers often used to worry about their daughters' welfare during this particular ritual. And with good reason, too! Apart from the obvious attractions, there are also sound historical reasons for this seasonal revival in lusty pursuits. The winter months provided a poor diet, especially in rural areas, and the addition of fresh food to meals in spring had a stimulating effect on the local lads. After gathering their boughs, the lads would adorn the village maids with garlands – which is why May Day was often referred to as 'Garland Day'. The young folk then returned to the village, and under cover of darkness each house was adorned with sprigs and greenery.

In many villages this was also used as an occasion to make a sly comment on the inhabitant of the house. The adornment chosen had a secret rhyming meaning – such as thorn for scorn, lime for prime, and pear blossom for fair (either of face or character). Holly or plum stood for folly or glum, and nutwood meant the inhabitant was regarded as a slut. To this day the villagers of Wishford in Wiltshire still bring green branches from the woods and adorn their houses. Although this particular rite is now carried out on Oak Apple Day (May 29th), the records show the custom was observed in Wishford in Tudor times, well before the inauguration of Oak Apple Day – indicating that it was originally a May Day custom.

May Day celebrations involve several traditional characters. To this day May Queens are elected throughout the land; and on the Isle of Man the May Queen used to have a ritual battle with the dying Queen of Winter. Another traditional character was Jack-in-the-Green. This part was usually taken by the local chimney sweep, who was dressed from head to toe in green foliage. Hobby-horses were also a regular feature, usually accompanied by Morris dancers. To this day a hobby-horse does the rounds in Minehead in Somerset, and in Padstow in Cornwall they have a special 'Obby Oss' who capers through the streets on May Day. In former times he ended up by frolicking in the local pond and splashing the villagers with water – almost certainly a remnant of some old rain-making rite. Nowadays he is expected to canter from house to house, frequently 'dying' – only to be revived by his accompanying 'teaser'. This too is probably a remnant of some ancient rite connected with the resurrection of Spring.

Many ancient May Day customs lapsed when the joyous and often lusty revels were banned by Cromwell and his Puritans. Afterwards several of the revived ceremonies came to be celebrated on Oak Apple Day, which marked the Restoration of Charles II. Other May Day celebrations were displaced when the calendar was changed in 1752. This accounts for the fact that the famous Furry Dance at Helston in Cornwall (originally a May Day celebration) is now held on the nearest Saturday to May 8th. In Cornish dialect 'furry' is synonymous with 'floral', and this is the dance which accompanies the well-known song 'All together in the floral dance . . . '. The dancers dress in their best clothes and wear posies of flowers (usually lilies of the valley). The dance goes on all day, and the dancers proceed down the streets and into the open doorways and through the houses. This is said to bring good luck to the household.

Recently the villagers of Helston have also taken to staging a play, called the 'Hal-an-Tow'. This is a revival of the old custom of May Day mumming plays, and the Helston performances feature several of the traditional characters who originally took part in these plays. These include Robin Hood (who is associated with Jack-in-the-Green), Little John, St George, and, in Helston, a unique local character called Aunt Mary Rose (whose part in other villages would have been taken by Maid Marion).

A distinctive feature of May Day is that it remains exclusively a pagan celebration. Whereas Christianity managed to absorb many of the ancient rites which occurred around Christmas and Easter, on May Day there was no appropriate Christian feast. An apparent exception here is the singing of Latin hymns on the top of the tower of

Magdalen College, Oxford, which is performed at sunrise every May Day. Once the singing is finished Morris dancers disperse to perform dances at various places throughout the city. The origin of this probably stems from the inaugural ceremony which was performed when the tower was completed in 1509, though this is far from certain.

Being a pagan celebration, May Day has naturally attracted its fair share of superstitions. May Day children are said to be unlucky; and in the Isles of Orkney and Shetland it was even customary to drown cats and chickens which were born on this day. The origin of this superstition has long been lost. Another May Day superstition decrees that May Day dew is a cure for many ills – especially if gathered from

'Obby Oss', Padstow

the graves of the recent dead. To bathe one's face in May Day dew is said to cure freckles and warts. Despite banning other May Day rites, Oliver Cromwell is said to have secretly believed in, and even practised, this one! And Samuel Pepys records his wife getting up in the middle of the night and going off into the country with a friend on the pretext of bathing her face in May Dew – though there is no record of the lusty diarist using this excuse to absent himself from the marriage bed!

Throughout the world May Day has also become associated with populist and socialist political demonstrations. In London, there is usually a procession from Speaker's Corner in Hyde Park which is addressed by leaders of the Labour Party.

From Spring to Summer's But a Day

At your service, sire

Oak Apple Day (May 29th) celebrates Charles II's triumphant entry into London after his Restoration in 1660. The name itself derives from that romantic episode when Charles was on the run from the Roundhead troops after the Battle of Worcester and hid in an oak tree at Boscobel. In past centuries it was customary to 'wear the oak' on this day, and everything from fishing boats to coaches and railway engines would be adorned with a sprig of oak leaves. Nowadays the main celebration takes place at the Royal Chelsea Hospital in London, home of the famous red-coated 'Chelsea Pensioners'. This Hospital was founded as a home for old soldiers in 1682 by Charles II, reputedly at the suggestion of Nell Gwynne, and their Founder's Day celebrations include a parade and march-past of the Pensioners, all resplendent with their medals and sprigs of oak leaves. Also the Hospital's statue of Charles II is covered with oak boughs – which besides its obvious symbolism is also probably an echo of the old Jack-in-the-Green May Day custom.

In previous centuries, when Oak Apple Day was more widely celebrated, it absorbed a number of ceremonies and traditions associated with the ancient cult of the oak which had a deep pre-Christian significance. This day was also once known as 'Pinch-Bum Day', and anyone found not wearing a sprig of oak was liable to get his or her bottom pinched – or in some cases to be showered with water, beaten with nettles, or even pelted with rotten eggs. This custom was observed from Cumberland to Cornwall, but gradually lapsed with the coming of the Industrial Revolution. Even this quaint custom is said to have its origins in historical fact. The story goes that when Charles was hiding in the oak he was so tired that he kept nodding off and almost falling out of the tree. So to keep him awake his faithful attendant had to keep pinching his bottom!

In previous centuries the month of May contained many rural celebrations. The reasons for this are both religious and practical. Ascension Day, Whitsun and Rogation Day are all liable to fall in May. (Though their actual dates are not fixed, being dependent upon Easter.) Also, by May most of the crops had been sown, and the cattle and sheep were all out grazing in the new pastures, which meant that this was a comparatively easy period in the rural calendar. Even in this age of industrial farming May and June are still the months when most 'businessmen-farmers' take their holidays.

Nowadays almost all of the ancient rural celebrations at this time of year have lapsed. In their place we have Whitsun fairs and regattas, together with that most English of ceremonies – the opening of the cricket season, which takes place everywhere from county cricket grounds overlooked by centuries-old cathedrals to humble village greens. An apocryphal yarn links this sporting evening to one of mankind's most ancient rituals. According to the story a formerly French African nation which was plagued with drought decided to despatch a team of local experts to discover why our land was so blessed with rain. Eventually the team returned home, having discovered the secret of our successful rain-making ritual. They reported that in villages throughout the land six sticks would be set up in the middle of a large field. Two men in white coats then entered the field and took up ceremonial positions. They were then followed by eleven attendants all clad completely in white, who also took up ceremonial positions. Finally, two men with ritual wooden clubs would emerge from a special wooden hut – whereupon the heavens would immediately open and the rains would fall in abundance.

One of the few **Whitsuntide** ceremonies which is still performed is the celebrated Dunmow Flitch trial, which takes place on Whit Monday at Great Dunmow, Essex. Here a flitch (a side of bacon) is offered to any couple that have been married for over a year and a day and can promise that they have never quarrelled or once 'sleeping or waking' wished to part.

Originally the contestants were 'tried' before a jury consisting of the Prior and villagers of Little Dunmow, though now the jury consists of six bachelors and six spinsters. In jovial Bank Holiday spirit the contesting couples are asked all manner of questions designed to test their claim – before the winners are finally awarded their flitch. This 'trial' goes back at least as far as the 13th century, when it is said to have been founded by a certain Robert Fitzwalter. The ceremony is mentioned by Chaucer and also in *Piers Plowman*, where it is recorded that 'since the plague hundreds of couples have married, yet the only fruit they have brought forth are foul words. . . . If they went to try for the Dunmow Flitch they would not stand a chance without the Devil's help'. Formerly this trial was taken very seriously, and for many years no award would be made at all. Indeed, before the Reformation there are records of only three such awards, despite the fact that until recently only the husband was required to give evidence. Records of similar customs have been found as far afield as Vienna and Brittany, though the Dunmow Flitch trial is the only authentic ceremony extant.

Another Whitsuntide ritual which now survives only in the villages of Derbyshire is the Well-Dressing Ceremony. In this the stone superstructures of the wells are dressed with flowers, moss and greenery to depict a scene from the Bible. The vicar then leads a procession, complete with brass bands, from well to well – where a service is held to bless each well for producing pure water throughout the previous year. The Well-Dressing Ceremony at the village of Tissington, Derbyshire is held on **Ascension Day** and, according to local tradition, this originates from 1350 when the village held a thanksgiving for having been spared from the Black Death which had raged throughout the area during the previous year. Other Well-Dressing Ceremonies are held on different days at Etwall and Wirksworth and several nearby villages.

Once upon a time there was an entire mythology of wells. In pre-Christian days wells and springs were regarded as sacred, and were thought to have their own special nymph or water sprite. Certain wells were believed to have magical or curative powers, and it is from this belief that the idea of 'holy' wells sprang up. These were particularly prevalent in the Celtic regions of Cornwall and Devon. It is from this that we get the superstition of 'Wishing Wells', with the custom of throwing coins into pools and fountains.

A strange Ascensiontide custom is celebrated in Boyes Staith at Whitby in Yorkshire. Here a hedge

(or horngarth) is erected along the low water mark in the harbour each year on May 26th. This custom is called 'Planting the Penny Hedge Horngarth', and it dates from 1159. Originally it was a penance imposed by the local Abbot on three local noblemen who had been hunting without permission and come across the local hermit at his prayers. After taunting the holy man they had eventually beaten him up – and to pay for their sins they were made to cut staves and osiers from a local wood and erect a fence along the seashore strong enough to withstand three high tides.

Rogationtide comes in the fifth week after Easter. The word 'Rogation' comes from the Latin word *rogare* – to ask or beseech – and the ceremonies attached to this day are concerned with asking for God's blessing on the newly planted crops. When this was an open-air ceremony conducted in the fields it was also used as an occasion to mark the parish boundaries. This custom almost certainly derives from the celebrations accorded to the Roman god Terminus, who was the god of fields and landmarks. In the days before maps the marking of parish boundaries was of great practical significance, and the *'Beating of the Bounds'* was a serious business. This custom still persists in many parishes, and even in the cities of Leicester and London – where the Tower of London ceremony dates back to 1555.

Nowadays the parish boundaries, or more usually the boundary stones, are beaten by choirboys with canes – a ritual observed with boisterous glee. However, in former centuries these boys

Well-dressing at Tissington, Derbyshire

would have been less happy to take part in the ritual – for in those days it was the boys themselves who were beaten! The idea here was to impress upon the youngsters the limits of their parish in a way that they wouldn't forget, and beside the beatings the ritual frequently consisted of throwing the boys into boundary streams, bramble bushes and patches of gorse at the edges of the parish. As part of the religious ceremonies attached to Rogation Day a passage from the Gospels would be read beneath an oak tree – the origin of naming certain districts 'Gospel Oak'.

High Days and Holidays

In prehistoric times **Midsummer's Day** was one of the most important days in the calendar. This was the longest day in the year, the day when the sun reached its highest point in the heavens before beginning the long descent into winter and the seemingly endless nights of darkness and fear. When Stonehenge was built, some time between 1900 and 1400 BC, its entire structure was orientated towards the rising of the sun at the summer solstice on June 21st. A millennium and a half later, when he began his campaigns in Gaul, Julius Caesar

25

recorded how the Druids and the Celtic tribes commemorated their god Taranis on this day. A large wickerwork cage would be constructed, and then filled with ritual victims. The cage would then be set on fire as a sacrifice to the god.

According to many historians this is the origin of Midsummer Bonfires – a custom which was once prevalent all over the country, and is still popular in Cornwall. These are now known as 'St John's Eve Midsummer Bonfires', and tradition has it that originally the fires were lit in an attempt to increase the power of the sun after Midsummer's Day, and also to banish the devils, spirits, ghosts and hobgoblins which were said to 'fly abroad this night to hurt mankind'. The ashes of these fires are sometimes ritually preserved to serve as a foundation for the next year's fire,

though happily the use of human beings as combustible material is no longer considered necessary to appease the gods! Yet this element is almost certainly echoed in the practices of Guy Fawkes Night, which has now attracted most of the ancient fire customs. Until well into the last century effigies were burnt on Midsummer Bonfires in villages and towns throughout the land from Bradford to Salisbury.

In Cornish villages it is considered lucky for couples to leap through the flames of Midsummer Bonfires, and when there is dancing round the fire this must always be done in a clock-wise direction, thus apparently following the sun on its course from East to West. In Devon, until recently there was a revived tradition of lighting bonfires on the tops of the high tors of Dartmoor on Midsummer's Eve.

Druid ceremony at Stonehenge

This was said to be in memory of the warning beacons which were lit to mark the arrival of the Spanish Armada in the 16th century, though in fact this too almost certainly had its origins in far older practices. This would seem to be confirmed by the old Devon tradition which said that if you stand on a high hill on Midsummer's Eve you can tell your fortune from the number of fires you can see and the appearance of the flames.

Midsummer Fires were once prevalent all over Europe, and in certain areas such as the Pyrenees and Hungary the tradition still survives. In Sweden Midsummer's Eve is one of the great occasions of the year, with young people dancing around maypoles and bonfires in the 'Midnight Sun'.

At Whalton in Northumberland they have a custom called 'Baal Fire', which involves the lighting of a bonfire on the village green. Although this takes place on July 4th, it is certainly an ancient Midsummer solstice bonfire – this being the old-style Midsummer's Eve before the change in the calendar in 1752.

A large body of superstitions has become attached to **Midsummer's Eve**, though most of these have now died out. According to one superstition, if you stay on your church porch through the night of Midsummer's Eve you will see pass before you the souls of all those who will die in the village during the following year. Though the Church officially disapproved of such superstitions, it is recorded that one Yorkshire sexton would regularly keep this vigil – just so that he could calculate his income from grave-digging during the year to come! Another Midsummer superstition, still remembered by old folk in Devon and Cornwall, is that a rose picked on Midsummer's Day will not lose its petals until Christmas. Also, if any girl places this rose under her pillow at night it is said that she will dream of her future husband. How the petals could survive until Christmas with such treatment is undisclosed.

Midsummer folklore is also attached to particular localities. A revival of the mystical Druid ceremony is still celebrated by the Most Ancient Order of Druids as the sun rises over the Heel Stone at Stonehenge. This ceremony is now attended by hundreds of people each year, and attracts visitors from all over the world. Another megalithic monument associated with Midsummer folklore is at Stanton Drew in Avon. Here the origin of the local circles of stones is explained by the Legend of the Devil's Wedding. According to the story a fiddler was playing for the dancers at an open-air wedding feast here on Midsummer's Eve, but when midnight tolled he refused to continue playing because it was the Sabbath. The bride became angry and demanded more music, even if it meant going to hell to pay for it. At once, an old man appeared and took the reluctant fiddler's place. He then started to play and the dancers continued, but as he went on playing the music became faster and faster, until finally the dancers sank to the ground in exhaustion. Then, as the cock crowed the fiddler vanished and the dancers were all turned into stone. According to the legend, this was all witnessed by the righteous fiddler, who stayed hidden under a nearby bush.

Midsummer's Eve is one of the most promising nights of the year for those wishing to encounter fairies and witches. At several spots on the South Downs in Sussex fairies are said to appear and dance in the moonlight on Midsummer's Eve. Most of these spots are near prehistoric earthworks or flint mines. However, there is no evidence of prehistoric activity at the nearby old oak tree in Broadwater where, according to local legend, on Midsummer's Eve a group of skeletons emerges and dances around the tree until dawn – doubtless providing a diverting interlude for the locals on their way home from the nearby inn.

Other superstitions attached to Midsummer's Eve are found from Cornwall to the Shetlands, and range from seals being transformed into singing maidens to cattle going down on their knees at midnight to pray. And at Appleton in Cheshire there's a custom called 'Bawming the Thorn', which takes place on July 5th, the old Midsummer's Eve. The thorn tree in the middle of the town is dressed with garlands and ribbons and dancing takes place. The present thorn tree was only planted in 1967, but the one it replaced was said to have been

grown from a cutting taken from the famous Holy Thorn of Glastonbury and planted in Appleton by one Adam de Dutton in 1125.

All the Fun of the Fair

Midsummer and the approach of harvest time was traditionally the time of country fairs, and these are still popular summer events throughout the country. Many of them used to be held on **St James's Day** (July 25th). In medieval times, St James was one of the most popular saints, and a pilgrimage to his shrine at Santiago de Compostela in northern Spain was considered an alternative for those who were unable or unwilling to brave the dangers of a full pilgrimage to the Holy Land. The pilgrims would return wearing a scallop shell in their caps, the scallop being the emblem of the saint. One outcome of this custom was the building of grottoes made of sea shells at the St James's Day Fairs, and an echo of this is to be found in the shell grottoes which remain at several of the older market towns by the sea on the south coast.

A curious St James's Day custom is still celebrated at the Horn Fair in the Sussex village of Evernhoe. Here the local cricket team plays against a neighbouring village, and while the match is being played a whole sheep is roasted. Afterwards the sheep is eaten, and the batsman who has scored the most runs for the winning side is presented with the horns. Though this custom involves a cricket match its origins are almost certainly older than the game, the horns probably being associated with some ancient rite involving male prowess.

The arrival of August brings

Lammas-tide, the ancient holiday which eventually became the original August Bank Holiday. There are various theories as to the origin of the word 'Lammas'. According to one, it is derived from 'Lamb Mass' (in ancient times, this was the service when the tithe lambs were presented to the church). Another, more generally accepted theory, has 'Lammas' deriving from the Anglo-Saxon word *hlaf-maesse*, which means 'loaf mass'. This was the feast when the sacramental bread was made from the first corn of the year's harvest. Another curious connection is with the ancient Celtic Quarter Day of Lugnasad. Lugh was an important Celtic god, and is commemorated in several place names in Celtic Europe. The French city of Lyons was once called Lugnudum, and the name London may have a similar derivation. The second half of the Celtic word, *-nasad*, stands for a tribal gathering where games took place. So it seems that Lugnasad was also a festival marking the start of the harvest.

Naturally enough, old Lammas (or Lugnasad) customs tended to persist longer in the Celtic areas of Britain, notably the Scottish Highlands and the Isle of Man. On the Isle of Man, Lammas-tide customs became an excuse for a certain amount of bacchanalian behaviour. According to local tradition, people would climb to the top of Snaefell, the highest peak on the island, and here they would behave 'very rudely and indecently'. The Church made great efforts to stamp out this custom, but all to no avail. However, it was the ingenuity of a certain Methodist minister which finally put a stop to these revels. On the appointed day, he decided to hold a service on the top of Snaefell – and all who reached the top were not only expected to take part in the service, but also to contribute to the collection box.

One of the more curious and sinister legends attached to Lammas-tide has to do with King William II, 'William Rufus', who met his death in the New Forest in 1100 on August 2nd, the day after Lammas Day. Some historians believe that his 'accidental' death was in fact an act of ritual sacrifice to the old gods during the time of Lugnasad.

Lammas-tide was also a great time for fairs, especially sheep fairs. The great three-day fair at Trowbridge in Wiltshire was mentioned by Thomas Hardy, and throughout the rural counties flocks of sheep would converge on the market towns. Many of these Lammas Day Fairs have been displaced, and the Lammas Fair in Exeter now takes place in the middle of July.

Attached to this fair is an ancient custom in which two sergeants-at-mace emerge from the Guildhall on the morning of the fair, one of them carrying a pole decorated with flowers and a large stuffed white glove. The sergeants-at-mace visit various parts of the city and read out a proclamation announcing that the Lammas Fair is to be held. When they return to the Guildhall the pole with the white glove is put on display. This is a symbol for the royal protection of the peace of the fair, and is said to derive from a charter issued by Edward I in the 13th century granting all traders freedom from arrest or confiscation of their goods whilst journeying to and from the fair.

A popular saint associated with this time of year is **St Swithun**, whose day falls on July 15th. According to the well-known rhyme:

St Swithun's Day, if thou be fair,
For forty days it will remain.
St Swithun's Day, if thou bring rain,
For forty days it will remain.

This association of St Swithun with rain derives from an ancient legend concerning the original St Swithun, who was Bishop of Winchester from 852 to 862. When he died, St Swithun requested that he should be buried outside the cathedral, for he wished the rainwater from the eaves of the cathedral to fall on his grave. However, when the cathedral was rebuilt a century later the monks decided to place his tomb inside the cathedral. The result was that on July 15th, 971, the day set aside for his reinterment, it started to rain. And for the next forty days the city and the surrounding countryside were inundated with downpours and great storms, which was deemed to indicate the displeasure of St Swithun at this disregard of his final wishes.

A ceremony that was once celebrated throughout the land at this time of year was the Rushbearing Ceremony, which was usually held on or around the feast of St Oswald (August 5th). Until the 18th century the floors of most churches consisted of beaten earth or flag-stones. These were covered with rushes, which served much the same purpose as our modern carpets, except that the rushes had to be renewed in a general clear-out once a year. These Rushbearing Ceremonies were prevalent until late into the last century over much of the north of England, where they often became linked with the Wakes Weeks in the industrial towns; and Rushbearing services are still held at several churches in the Lake District at this time of year, though the bringing of the rushes is now wholly symbolic.

However, what all this has to do with St Oswald remains a mystery. St Oswald was a 7th-century king of Northumbria who achieved great success in battle after being converted to Christianity, where-upon he decided to convert all whom he defeated. Unfortunately, in the eighth year of his reign he himself was finally defeated by the king of Mercia, who ordered his body to be savagely mutilated. However, despite these indignities St Oswald's head was eventually deposited in the tomb of St Cuth-bert in 875. At the end of the 10th century the remains of St Cuthbert were deposited in Durham Cathed-ral; and it was here, over 1000 years after his death, that the head of St Oswald was finally rediscovered in 1827.

This is the time of year when the Wakes Weeks used to be celebrat-ed, especially in the north of Eng-land. Strictly speaking a wake is just another form of feast, and can occur at any time of year; but in the industrial towns of Yorkshire and Lancashire Wakes Week was the annual holiday when the mills and factories all closed down and every-one who could went off to the sea-side. The word 'wake' in fact means 'vigil', and comes from the centur-ies-old custom of 'Waking' (or stay-ing awake) in the local church the night before a holy day.

In medieval times most villages celebrated their annual wakes or feasts on the saint's day' of their

Mead

Mead is still manufactured commercially and it's worth having a glass if you encounter it. To be honest, it's very sweet and not something you'd want to drink in any quantity. If you're feeling patient, why not make it yourself?

3½lb (1.75kg) honey
8 pints (5 litres) water
1oz (30g) yeast

Boil the honey and water together for 1 hr, skimming very carefully. Drain the skimmings through a sieve and return the liquid to the saucepan. When almost cold add the yeast. Leave in a cool place. Bottle and drink in a year's time.

local church: thus village wakes were liable to occur at any time of year. However, in 1536 an Act of Convention decreed that every parish should celebrate its wake on the first Sunday in October. As with many other attempts at imposing bureaucratic conformity this was soon forgotten, with most parishes quickly reverting to their favoured saint's day.

Another of the great fair days at this time of year was **St Bartholomew's Day** on August 24th. The best known of these fairs was the famous Bartholomew Fair at Smithfield in London, which was held for over 700 years from the reign of Henry I until 1855. This was largely a holiday and commercial fair, and it was not especially devoted to the wares of the great meat market. During the Middle Ages it was the most important cloth fair in England, at a time when much of the country's wealth was generated by this trade. By the 16th century the fair extended over a fortnight, and featured many different forms of entertainment, several of which are celebrated in Ben Jonson's *Bartholomew Fair*. At this time, Smithfield was also London's main site for execution, and during the short reign of Mary Tudor (1553–8) over 250 Protestants were burnt at the stake here.

In Cornwall, St Bartholomew is especially revered as the patron saint of beekeepers and honey makers. For centuries St Bartholomew played a central role in the Blessing of the Mead by the monks at Gulval, near Mount's Bay, where his blessing was called upon by an official with the splendiferous title 'The Alderman of the Fraternity of St Bartholomew of the Craft of Mystery of Free Mead-makers of Great Britain and Ireland'.

St Bartholomew's Fairs are still held at Carlisle and Newbury; and in West Wilton in Yorkshire, where the local church is called St Bartholomew's, they construct a large straw effigy called 'Bartle', who is carried through the streets while the villagers chant a traditional local rhyme:

> At Pen Hill crags he tore his rags
> At Hunter's Thorn he blew his horn
> At Capplebank Stee he brak his knee
> At Grassgill Beck he brak his neck
> At Waddam's End he couldn't fend
> At Grassgill End he met his end.

After this, the effigy is stabbed and set on fire. A strange treatment for a saint! However, it seems that on this occasion the saint has become identified with a notorious thief who was caught centuries ago in the village at this time of year. Once again there would appear also to be an echo here of the old Midsummer Bonfire rites.

Hip-hip for Harvest!

Come, ye thankful people, come,
Raise the song of harvest home:
All is safely gathered in,
Ere the winter storms begin.

In bygone centuries the gathering of the harvest was the important economic and social event of the year. A bad harvest spelt ruin, starvation, and even death – whilst a good harvest was a cause for rejoicing. Though the harvest is no longer all-important in our modern industrial age, **Harvest Home Festivals** are still celebrated in churches throughout the land. The main feature is usually a display of seasonal fruit and vegetables which is arranged in the church for the Sunday service; and even if nowadays much of this produce comes from the local supermarket, an atmosphere of thanksgiving prevails, especially in rural areas where harvest yields still matter.

Naturally, with an activity of such vital concern, all manner of superstitions grew up around harvest practices. Popular belief had it that the Last Sheaf of the harvest contained the Corn Spirit, and the man who cut it was said to kill her. In consequence, it was thought to bring bad luck if you were the reaper of the last sheaf. On some farms, this last sheaf was always left standing, whilst on others the harvesters would draw lots for who was to cut it down. When the loser had cut the sheaf he would be set upon in boisterous fashion by his assembled mates, often being given 'the bumps' in a rug. However, this apparently harmless practice harks back to a more savage ritual. In pre-Christian times the Last Reaper was sometimes ceremonially sacrificed as soon as he had completed his task – only this, it was said, would restore the Corn Spirit to life so she could rise again next year.

When the last sheaf had been cut, it was a custom to raise it into the air and break into the old Harvest Shout, one version of which runs:

Well ploughed,
Well sowed,
Well harrowed,
Well mowed,
And all safely carted to the barn wi'
  nary a load throwed!
Hip-hip-hip-hooray!

Corn dolly making

After this, it was customary to make the last sheaf into a tiny figure, known as a 'Corn Dolly', or 'Kern Baby'. In Scotland this was known as 'the Maiden', if the harvest was gathered early, or 'the Cailleach' (meaning old hag) if the harvest was gathered late. The corn dolly was usually woven into an intricate design resembling a human figure, and the making of corn dollies was a folk art requiring considerable skill, though sometimes the corn dolly would merely be made in the shape of a pyramid or miniature wheatsheaf. The corn dolly would usually be made on the spot, as soon as the last sheaf had been cut. It would then be brought home in a triumphant procession where it was given a place of honour at the Harvest Supper. When the rejoicing was over the corn dolly would be kept on a shelf until Plough Monday in January, when it would be ritually reinterred under the turf from the first furrow.

In some cases a communal corn dolly would be made for the entire parish, and this would be hung

from a pew in the local church at the Harvest Festival service. This practice is still carried out at Whalton in Northumbria and Little Waltham in Essex. In many other parishes the corn dolly is hung in the church porch.

Nowadays there has been a revival of the ancient art of making corn dollies; and though they no longer have quite the same ritual significance, their intricacy and ingenuity of design makes them into pleasant original decorations in many country homes.

Bringing the last sheaves of the harvest home was traditionally an occasion of great rejoicing and merriment. The horses which drew the cart were frequently adorned with garlands and the cart was decorated with greenery and flowers. In many districts it was customary for the man who drove the cart to dress as a woman. And on the way home the tired harvesters would often sing special harvest songs, such as:

Harvest Home! Harvest Home!
We've ploughed, we've sown,
We've ripped, we've mown,
Harvest Home! Harvest Home!
We want water and kain't get none!

And after the men had sung the last line the girls would shower them with pails of water.

Surprisingly, the tradition of Harvest Festival services in parish churches is a comparatively modern custom. It is said to have been started in 1843 by the Vicar of Morwenstow in Cornwall, the renowned Rev. R. S. Hawker, who revived it in connection with a late celebration of the lapsed Lammastide festival. According to the story, the idea soon became so popular that it quickly spread all over the country. However, it is almost certain that religious observances connected with harvest thanksgiving existed in some form long before this in many areas – even if, before this date, the main celebrations were usually in the fields and at the Harvest Supper.

After the long toil of gathering in the harvest (which each day began early in the morning and often lasted until the dew came down late in the night), the Harvest Supper was invariably a fairly boisterous affair. In the West Country and the Midlands the traditional Harvest Home Supper consisted of boiled beef and carrots, plum pudding and ale, and bread baked in the shape of an ear of wheat. In the apple counties, cider would be drunk instead of ale, and often the meat course would consist of a large rabbit pie filled with all the rabbits which had been shot in the fields during the harvest. One part of the meal did not vary: it seems that throughout the land it was traditional to eat plum pudding.

An indication of the atmosphere at these suppers is given by the old Harvest Supper tradition of 'Turnover', which was popular all over southern England. In this ritual, each participant is given a top hat, on which he has to balance a mug of ale or cider. He then has to down his mug of ale without touching it with his hands. Meanwhile the assembled company sings:

I've bin to Plymouth, and I've bin to Dover;
I've bin a-ramblin' the whole world over,
Over and over and over and over.
Drink up your liquor and turn your cup over,
Over and over and over and over,
The liquor's drink'd up and the cup is turned over.

34

As soon as the drinker has emptied his mug, he has to toss it in the air, turn the top hat right way up, and catch the mug inside the brim. If he doesn't manage to complete this ritual successfully before the company has finished the song, his penance is to go through the whole ritual all over again until he finally manages to complete it properly, or he falls to the floor incapable!

In other parts of the country similar boisterous rituals were enacted to the general merriment of the company, and it was traditional for prodigious amounts of ale to be consumed by all concerned. Indeed, in Hertfordshire the day after Harvest Supper was always considered a public holiday, and was known appropriately enough as 'Drinking Day'.

Not surprisingly, these harvest celebrations often got out of hand, and in many parts of the country this time of year was notorious for the settling of old scores and public brawls. This tendency was often exacerbated by the employment of casual or itinerant labour. In the villages, the local carpenter, publican and blacksmith and even the schoolmaster were all expected to join in. During the 19th century, work gangs building the railways through the countryside would often down tools to join in the harvest, and itinerant families and gypsies were frequently co-opted to lend a hand. Inevitably, any frictions or suspicions which had built up during the long hard days in the corn fields all came to a head at the harvest celebrations.

The practice of employing seasonal itinerant labour was common all over the cider counties at apple harvest time, and during the slack

months these families would often make a living potato picking. In Kent, it was the tradition for the hops to be picked by families of Cockneys from the East End of London, who came to regard this jaunt into the countryside as their annual holiday. Sometimes families would return generation after generation to the same farm, and after the day's work a good time would be had by all – often too good a time by some, with the result that unexpected babies born nine months later were known as 'Hop kids' (and if they were taken to the foundling home they were traditionally given the surname Hopkins!). Only in the last decades, with the advent of mechanical harvesters, has this form of holiday-making for urban workers finally died out.

Michaelmas Goose and Tawdry Goods

After harvest time, the next great event in the traditional calendar is **Michaelmas**, on September 29th. Traditionally tenancies on farms ran from Michaelmas to Michaelmas; and as this was the time when the tenancies ran out, throughout the country there were big fairs for selling off the livestock of those who were abandoning the land, as well as for hiring of new labour.

This was also the time of the great Sheep Fairs, such as the Wilton Great Fair in Wiltshire. In the middle of the last century over 100,000 sheep would change hands here every year. At Weyhill in Hampshire, there has been a Michaelmas Fair since the time of the Norman Conquest, though nowadays this is held on October 10th (the old Michaelmas Day according to the pre-1752 calendar). Tradition has it that this fair first took place at the crossroads where the ancient Tin Road from Cornwall to London met the Gold Road from Ireland to Dover, though this remains unverified. According to the records, at the end of the last century over £300,000 was spent on sheep each year at this fair – and in those days you could often buy a sheep for half a guinea (52½p).

These sheep fairs would often be so large that they would look like complete makeshift villages, with rows of pens and tents, booths and stalls. Amidst all the commotion and bustle it's not surprising that the fairs became notorious for all kinds of villainy and sharp practice. The visiting shepherds even evolved their own picturesque but practical custom of sleeping in circles with their feet pointing outwards and their heads pillowed on their sheepdogs, their most valued possession.

Even some of the established customs associated with these fairs were fairly tough. On the eve of the Wilton Great Fair a traditional contest was held for the title 'King of the Shepherds'. Despite its name, this title had nothing to do with pastoral expertise – the contests being all-in fights with cudgels, involving wrestling, kicking, punching and even biting. Similar contests were held at most sheep fairs, though most of the others evolved definite local rules, and the fights were usually stopped either when a contestant was cudgelled to the ground or when the first blood was drawn.

Besides sheep, this time of year is also associated with geese. In earlier times, it was the custom to let the geese 'go a-stubbling' – which meant letting them roam in the fields after harvest to glean any leftover ears of corn and fallen grain. By Michaelmas, the geese would be well fattened, and in many parts of the country it was the custom to eat the Stubble Geese on Michaelmas Day. In some areas, though, it was the custom to give this Michaelmas Goose to the landlord when paying the rent – as is remembered in the old rhyme:

> And when the tenants come to pay
> their quarter's rent,
> They bring some fowl at Michael-
> mas, a dish of fish at Lent,
> At Christmas a capon, at Michael-
> mas a goose,
> And something else at New Year's
> Eve for fear the lease fly loose.

The famous Nottingham Goose Fair used to start on October 2nd and go on for 21 days. A local story has it that the fair got its name when an old farmer brought his three grown-up sons to the market for the first time. The sons had lived all their life on a remote farm and were overawed by all they saw, especially when they caught sight of three pretty girls in their coloured dresses. 'Aw, them's just silly geese', replied their father, when they asked about the girls. So later, when the father asked his sons what they wanted to buy to take home

with them, the three of them replied as with one voice: 'I be wantin' a goose, father.'

Hatfield Fair is famous for its contribution to the English language. This fair used to be held on the feast day of the town's patron saint, Etheldreda, locally known as 'St Awdry'. Many of the knick-knacks sold at the fair were cheap and shoddy, and so in time they came to be given the nick-name 'tawdry' goods.

Because of the custom of hiring labourers at this time of year, many of the fairs were known as 'Hiring Fairs'. Labourers and servants seeking hire would stand in the main thoroughfare of the fair carrying or wearing an emblem of their trade. Shepherds would wear a tuft of wool or carry a crook, carters would carry whips, and maids would traditionally carry mops (which was why these fairs were sometimes known as 'Mop Fairs'). This practice often led to certain abuses and, according to a late-19th-century chronicler: 'Young girls dressed in their finest clothes were exhibited like cattle to be hired by the would-be employers, who came to the fair to seek their services, and the scenes which frequently took place at the close of days were too disgraceful for description.' Nor was this mere Victorian prudery for, as Thomas Hardy wrote, the future Mayor of Casterbridge actually sold his wife at one of these fairs.

According to a superstition which is still remembered in the West Country and parts of Wales, the Devil spits on all blackberries on Michaelmas Day, and any picked after this are no good either for eating or cooking.

Oft Seen in Autumn

There is a hugely popular custom which takes place at this time of year, and shows no sign of dying out. With the coming of early autumn the horse-chestnut trees begin shedding their shiny and attractive but inedible nuts, which are commonly called 'conkers'. As every schoolboy knows, the conker is pierced by a skewer and threaded on a string. The rules of conkers dictate that each of the two contestants takes it in turn to hit his opponent's conker with his own, while his opponent holds his conker dangling on its string. The first conker to shatter is the loser. Each conker starts with a numerical value of one, and the winner takes on the score of his opponent. Thus after two fresh conkers have fought, the winner has a score of two. But if this winner is in his turn defeated, the new winner adds two to his own score. In this way, especially hard and nobbly conkers can often achieve vast scores on school playgrounds, becoming objects of deep reverence or envy as the season progresses! Nowadays there is even a World Conker Championship. This is held every year at the Chequered Skipper Inn at Ashton, near Oundle in Northamptonshire, during the second week of October, when enthusiasts from all over the country bring their lovingly-hardened conkers to compete for a coveted silver cup.

Also popular at this time of year are edible chestnuts. Despite competition from hot dog and hamburger stalls, vendors of roasted chestnuts with their small brazier-like stands are still common on the streets of London and some provincial cities – a sight as familiar in

Victorian times as the itinerant Italian organ grinders, ginger beer merchants and watercress sellers, who have now disappeared. One persistent example of the travelling street vendor – found in London and other major cities and in the West Country – is the gypsy selling bunches of violets and sprigs of 'lucky' white heather.

Another street-selling tradition, which is unfortunately dying fast, is the autumn visit of the French onion sellers. A distinctive sight, they come over from Brittany with their bicycles and strings of onions dangling from the handlebars, returning year after year to their own particular 'patch'. Nowadays the few who keep up this custom are old men, and most of their sons have deserted the land for the big cities, or are more interested in driving a tractor and going on camping holidays to the South of France, rather than taking a working holiday in rainy autumn England.

Spirits and Spells

In the ancient Celtic calendar, early November was the beginning of the New Year. This festival was called 'Samhain', and marked the end of the harvest and the beginning of winter. Around this time animals were slaughtered and cured for the long months ahead. It was also customary to light the fire on the hearth, which would then burn continuously throughout the winter. This was also the time when the spirits of the dead were thought to return and wander abroad. As a

preventative measure the gods were appeased with a burnt sacrifice (often involving a human being), and torches from the bonfires were carried out into the night to chase away the dead before they could cast their spells.

Many of these customs are echoed in our present celebrations of Hallowe'en and Guy Fawkes Night. Of the two, **Hallowe'en** (October 31st) is now more popular in Ireland and the Roman Catholic areas of Scotland – where Guy Fawkes Night is not celebrated, owing to the fact that it commemorates a failed Roman Catholic plot.

In the West Country Hallowe'en is often known as 'Punkie Night'. The word 'punkie' comes from 'pumpkin', and the 'punkies' are lanterns made from hollowed-out pumpkins. A candle is placed inside the hollowed-out pumpkin and holes are carved into its skin to make a face, giving the pumpkin an eerie 'bogey-man' aspect. These Hallowe'en lanterns (or sometimes similar artefacts made of paper) are still popular with children all over the country, and are carried to Hallowe'en parties suspended on sticks. (At each house the children ask for candles, and it is considered bad luck to turn them away empty-handed.) Originally, the pumpkin lanterns were intended to represent the souls of the dead, with the idea of protecting those who carried them from risen spirits and the powers of evil.

Hallowe'en is traditionally the night when the spirits of the dead return to earth. A general atmosphere of evil is said to prevail, with witches flying through the night sky on broomsticks and holding their notorious Sabbath. Bonfires were lit at dusk to drive away these evil spectres and protect the living, and the assembled company would link hands and dance around the fire. At the end of these celebrations you had to race back to your house before the fire died down – for when the fire went out 'the Devil took the hindmost'.

When Queen Victoria stayed at Balmoral, it was customary on Hallowe'en to light a large bonfire outside the main door. Highlanders with bagpipes would play around the fire, and the effigy of an ancient witch called 'Shandy Dann' would be burnt after a long list of all her sins had been read out to the assembled company. In Scotland, it was also the custom to bake apples, potatoes and neeps (turnips) in the Hallowe'en bonfires, and if you were bold enough to leap through the flames this brought you luck.

In country districts throughout England, Hallowe'en was often known as 'Nutcrack Night', 'Crab-apple Night' or 'Apple and Candle Night' – these names referring to the traditional games involving nuts, apples and candles which were played around the fire. Many of these games are thought to have originated in the Celtic Samhain, the ancient Winter's Eve, and though most of these games are now no longer played, one old favourite still remains popular at fairs and fêtes throughout Britain (though it is usually played in the summer). This game is variously known as 'Apple Bobby' or 'Ducking for Apples'. A number of apples are floated in a tub of water; the contestants then have their hands tied behind their backs and try to catch one of the apples between their teeth. Sometimes nuts or

silver coins were substituted for the apples – the fact that these don't float merely adding to the fun. Other games involved catching apples suspended on strings and, in Scotland, bannocks covered in treacle. These games are thought to be remnants of the old divination rites carried out at Samhain, when people would try to discover what fate held in store for them during the coming year.

Nowadays Hallowe'en is usually celebrated with parties, which often include echoes of these traditional elements. Pumpkin lanterns are used as decoration, and the guests are often expected to come in fancy dress. The ladies usually dress as witches, or wear cat's whiskers (the black cat being the witch's traditional familiar), and the men come as ghosts, monsters of some kind, or wizards.

Also associated with Hallowe'en is Mischief Night, though in some areas this is now deemed to fall on Guy Fawkes Eve (November 4th). Observance of this night has largely died out, except in parts of the north of England. Customarily it is a kind of winter night's April Fool's Day, when young people indulge in all kinds of tricks – such as howling through letter boxes, or tying neighbouring front door-handles together – the idea being that on Mischief Night you can't be punished for any pranks. In the last century, Mischief Night was also celebrated in certain parts on May Eve and Shrove Tuesday. Nowadays, much of its spirit seems to have become absorbed into Guy Fawkes Night, with the throwing of squibs and thunderflashes taking the place of more traditional pranks.

Gurning contest, Egremont Crabapple Fair

Gunpowder, Treason and Plot

> Remember, remember,
> The fifth of November,
> Gunpowder Treason and Plot.
> I see no reason
> Why Gunpowder Treason
> Should ever be forgot.

We all know the old rhyme, but some of its regional variations are slightly less familiar. In Nottingham, for instance, the children chant:

> Gunpowder Plot
> Shall ne'er be forgot
> While Nottingham Castle
> Stands on its rock.

In Edinburgh, they substitute the name of their own castle; while in other parts of Scotland, they sing:

> Guy Fawkes, Guy,
> Poke him in the eye,
> Stick him up the chimney pot
> And there let him die.

As every schoolboy knows, **Guy Fawkes Night** commemorates the uncovering of the Gunpowder Plot in 1605 – when Guy Fawkes (really called Guido Fawkes) was discovered in the cellars of the Houses of Parliament on November 5th (in fact, in the early hours of the morning) with 36 barrels of gunpowder intended to blow up King James I when he arrived for the Opening of Parliament later in the day. For his part in the plot, Guy Fawkes was hanged, drawn and quartered – and though this event did not actually take place until the January of the following year, this is what is commemorated when 'Guys' are burned on bonfires throughout the land on November 5th, and in London alone over ten times that original amount of gunpowder is exploded in fireworks.

According to historians, the main reason why this anniversary celebration caught on so rapidly was that during the early 17th century Puritan influence was busily suppressing many of the old traditional festivals, and this excuse for a loyal celebration provided an ideal opportunity for a resurrection of the old festive spirit. In consequence, many of the ancient Hallowe'en and Samhain observances quickly became attached to Guy Fawkes Night. This celebration also provided an opportunity to give vent to a large amount of anti-Catholic feeling, particularly in areas which had suffered under Mary Tudor. Until recently, the Pope's effigy was burnt alongside the traditional Guy, especially in Lewes in Sussex and in parts of Scotland. And in Cambridgeshire, instead of 'Remember, remember . . . ' they used to chant around the fire:

> A rope, a rope, to hang the Pope,
> A piece of cheese to toast him,
> A barrel of beer to drink his health,
> And a right good fire to roast him.

Happily, these anti-Catholic sentiments have generally been long forgotten. Indeed, many Roman Catholic families in England now find no anomaly in joining in the celebrations of Guy Fawkes Night, which to all intents and purposes, has simply become a traditional national celebration. An early result of this transformation was the habit of burning, alongside Guy Fawkes, an effigy of some national enemy. Until the middle of the last century, a popular candidate for this position was a figure called 'Boney', representing Napoleon. During the Boer War effigies of Kruger, the Boer leader, were burnt; later on the Kaiser and Hitler took their turn.

Opposite: Guy. Overleaf: Edinburgh Festival Tattoo, Edinburgh Castle

On November 5th, no town or district is without its Guy Fawkes bonfire. This is usually accompanied by fireworks; though in some towns, especially in southern England, there is also a traditional torchlight procession. In Ottery St Mary, in Devon, they still go in for the old practice of tar-barrel rolling. Here, a barrel of tar is set on fire and carried for as long as the carrier can bear the heat. He then drops the barrel, whereupon it is taken up by another carrier, who runs as fast as he can to keep the growing flames streaming out behind him. Eventually the barrel becomes too hot to hold and is rolled down the street until it falls apart in a ball of flame. Each year this practice is repeated with nine barrels in turn, and is now so popular that there is even a junior barrel-rolling, held earlier in the evening with smaller barrels.

Another popular custom associated with Guy Fawkes is collecting 'pennies for the guy'. Children throughout the land construct their guys out of straw-filled pillow cases and old clothes, and then the guy is dragged through the streets on a wheel cart or in an old pram, with passers-by being asked to spare a penny for the guy. Unfortunately, this highly popular form of indiscriminate begging now tends to start many weeks before November 5th, and by late October there are few underground stations in London without some kind of ramshackle guy lying by the entrance surrounded by a horde of persistent attendants – many of whom tend to become extremely indignant when they are only offered a penny!

Tar barrel rolling, Ottery St Mary

Lest We Forget

Martinmas, sometimes known as 'St Martin's Day', falls on November 11th. Around this time of year there was often a brief spell of summery weather, which is still known in many country districts as 'St Martin's Summer'. In Scotland, this was the day when farm tenancies traditionally lapsed, and it was also the day set aside for the slaughter of animals before the winter.

However, after 1918 Martinmas became remembered on account of an entirely different slaughter, for after this it was better known as 'Armistice Day'. Throughout the land on November 11th services were held to remember the millions who had given their lives in the First World War. And just before 11 o'clock in the morning, the hour at which the Armistice was signed, sirens sounded and bells tolled all over the country to mark the start of a two-minute silence. All work ceased in offices and factories, cars and buses came to a halt, and on the streets passers-by stood in silence.

After the Second World War this Remembrance Day was transferred to the nearest Sunday to Martinmas, and was taken as an opportunity to commemorate the fallen in both World Wars. Remembrance services are still held throughout the land – most notably the service at the Cenotaph in Whitehall.

Later in the month comes the **Feast of St Cecilia**, on November 22nd. St Cecilia, a 3rd-century martyr of the early Roman church, is the patron saint of music; and it is customary in many places to hold special St Cecilia's Day concerts.

Gingerbread

Most regions have their own special recipes for this dark, thick, sticky delight. This recipe comes from Yorkshire. A close relation of gingerbread is *parkin*; like gingerbread it is best kept for a few weeks before eating, and it is traditionally eaten on Guy Fawkes Night. Grasmere Gingerbread, on the other hand, isn't like gingerbread at all. It's a Lake District delicacy more like a gingery shortbread.

10oz (300g) flour
1 tsp ground ginger
1/2 tsp ground cinnamon
pinch of salt
4 oz (125g) chopped dates
5 oz (150g) treacle
3 oz (90g) butter
1 egg, beaten
4 oz (125g) dark brown sugar
3/4 tsp bicarbonate of soda, dissolved in 3 tsp of milk

Sieve together the flour, ginger, cinnamon and salt. Add the dates. Melt the treacle and butter together over a gentle heat and leave to cool slightly. Beat together the egg and sugar. Add the butter and treacle to the flour alternately with the egg and sugar. Add the bicarbonate of soda and beat well until soft, adding a little water, if necessary. Pour into a lined, greased, square (10in, 25cm) cake tin.

Bake in a preheated oven 170°C (325°F or Mark 3) for 1 1/2 hrs.

Christmas Comes, and with it Cheer!

All our end-of-year celebrations stem from ancient rituals marking the winter solstice on December 22nd. This is the shortest day of the year, when the noon-day sun reaches its lowest point before its long ascent to midsummer. In primeval times, rituals aimed at ensuring that the sun would successfully begin this ascent were a prime feature of the winter solstice. However, psychologically it was also a time when some jollification was needed to break the tedium of the long dark winter.

Our present Yuletide and midwinter celebrations are a curious amalgamation of pagan and religious observances. The main festive days range from St Nicholas' Day (December 6th), through Christmas Day and Boxing Day, to New Year and Twelfth Night. The current customs of Christmas involve putting up decorations, the giving and receiving of presents, church services, carol singing, Christmas dinner, parties and Nativity plays. Other observances which have now largely lapsed included the burning of Yule Logs, the passing of the Wassail Bowl, and ancient Mumming Plays – one of whose traditional characters was St Nicholas, now better known as Santa Claus or Father Christmas.

Little is known of the original St Nicholas beyond the fact that he was probably a bishop in the Near East some time during the 4th century. In the Greek Orthodox and Roman Catholic churches he has long been known as the patron saint of children, his symbol being three bags of gold. The winter-clad appearance of Santa Claus – hardly appropriate for a native of the Near East – probably stems from the fact that St Nicholas was also the patron saint of Russia until, under communism, he was replaced by a figure who in many ways bears a curiously similar appearance. However, there are other, more ancient reasons why Santa Claus rides in a reindeer-driven sleigh carrying gifts. These attributes can be related to the ancient Norse god Wodin – whose name is still commemorated in the word Wednesday (Wodin's Day). Wodin was also known to ride through the sky at this time of year scattering gifts to his devotees, and with the coming of Christianity certain attributes of this banished pagan figure became amalgamated with St Nicholas.

The ancient ritual of wassailing has now been completely absorbed by our custom of carol singing. In former times a large wassail bowl would be filled with punch and taken from home to home by singing groups of villagers asking for alms. Nowadays, carol singing is exclusively a Christmas custom, though in former times carols were also sung at Easter.

Once upon a time the Yule Log was a prominent feature of Christmas celebrations. This was brought into the home on Christmas Eve and kindled with a faggot from the previous year's Yule Log. It was then kept alight throughout the festivities, serving as a communal fire. If for any reason the Yule Log went out this was said to be an extremely evil omen, and great efforts were made to keep the Yule Log burning, sometimes throughout the entire 12 days of Christmas. In Scotland, and many parts of Europe,

Carol singers, Long Wittenham, Berkshire

the ashes of the Yule Log were scattered over the fields as a fertility charm, or dropped into wells to purify the water, and sometimes they were even kept as a lucky charm against hailstones!

A common variant on the Yule Log practices was the custom of burning a large Yule Candle, which was also kept burning throughout the holiday. In some parts, the wick of the candle would be kept as a lucky charm – being lit again during thunderstorms to prevent the house from being struck by lightning.

Now all that remains of these Yule Log practices is the custom of making Christmas cakes in the shape of Yule Logs. However, other ancient domestic observances remain in the form of hanging up holly, ivy and mistletoe as decorations. Previously, holly was regarded as the haunt of woodland sprites, and the holly tree was called the 'Witches' Tree' – with the result that it was considered unlucky to bring these into the house before the sanctified time of Christmas Eve.

Likewise, mistletoe also has its pagan associations. This was the Golden Bough of Classical legend, and it was also sacred to the ancient Druids of the old Celtic religion. For some reason mistletoe has never lost its pagan associations, and according to ancient tradition is still not allowed into churches, though holly, ivy and other evergreens are considered quite acceptable. The origin of the custom of kissing under the mistletoe almost certainly derives from it being the old Norse plant of peace, when it served much the same purpose in battle as the modern white flag.

King George I's Christmas Pudding

Christmas Pudding is the greatest of the plum puddings. This majestic creation was served to King George I (sometimes known as the 'Pudding King') on his first Christmas Day in England in 1714.

12 oz (350g) shredded suet
8 oz (250g) stoned prunes
8 oz (250g) mixed peel
8 oz (250g) small raisins
8 oz (250g) seedless sultanas
8 oz (250g) currants
8 oz (250g) sifted self-raising flour
8 oz (250g) demerara sugar
8 oz (250g) breadcrumbs
4 oz (125g) dates
4 oz (125g) glacé cherries
1 tsp mixed spice
1/2 nutmeg, grated
1 tsp salt
6 eggs, beaten
1/2 pint (15cl) milk
juice of 1/2 lemon
large wine glass of brandy

Mix together the dry ingredients, stir in the eggs, and add the milk, lemon juice and brandy, mixed together. Leave to stand for 12 hrs in a cool place. Turn into 1 large and 2 small buttered basins. Cover each basin with foil and then wrap each one up in a muslin cloth. Stand each basin in a large saucepan and pour in sufficient water to come halfway up each bowl. Boil the puddings for 6 hrs, adding more boiling water from time to time.

On Christmas Day, boil for 2 hrs before serving. The puddings will keep for 2 years.

However, the full significance of hanging holly and ivy as Christmas decorations is now forgotten. The fact that these are evergreens is probably the most salient feature. They would have been emblematic of some kind of life continuing even in the midst of dark bare midwinter.

The custom of sending Christmas cards is comparatively recent. This started in the middle of the last century – though there are several claims as to the origin of the practice. In the British Museum there is a card designed by a schoolboy called William Egley in 1842, and this is generally considered as the earliest example of its kind.

The cult of Christmas cribs, a popular feature in churches and homes throughout the land at this time of year, is said to have been started by St Francis of Assisi in 1224. St Francis used a real manger filled with hay and a live ox and a donkey, and mass was celebrated over the manger on Christmas Eve.

However, the giving of gifts at Christmas time long precedes the advent of Christianity. In ancient Rome it was customary to exchange gifts at the Feast of the Saturnalia, the popular midwinter revels, and this custom was also practised at the Kalends of January, the New Year feast which began on January 1st. These customs were widespread throughout the Roman Empire, and the gifts themselves were thought to be omens, which meant special care was taken to choose presents which were golden or sweet, or symbolic of light. In early Christian times, though, these customs were shunned by all believers, since they were regarded as pagan practices. Only later was the giving of gifts accepted by Christians, when it became associated with the gifts of the Three Kings.

The tradition of putting up and decorating Christmas trees in the home originated in Germany. It is said to have been started by Martin Luther. When he was walking through a wood one Christmas night he noticed the stars glittering through the branches of a fir tree. This is said to have given him the idea of setting up a candlelit tree in his home for his children, to remind them of the starry heavens.

Unlike many Christmas customs Christmas trees were popular in America long before they reached England, being taken there by early German settlers, especially the socalled 'Pennsylvania Dutch' (who were not from Holland at all, but were in fact 'Deutsch'). The Christmas tree was first brought to these shores by Prince Albert, Queen Victoria's German consort. In 1841 the Royal Family celebrated Christmas around a lighted tree at Windsor Castle, and when this was reported in *The Times* the custom rapidly caught on. However, as with many 'firsts', there are disputing claimants. According to some chroniclers, the German merchants in Manchester had passed on this Christmas tree custom to their English neighbours early in the 19th century; and long before this there is even mention in medieval records of a decorated tree in the streets of London at Christmas time.

However, the idea of having communal Christmas trees in public places did not catch on either in Germany or in Britain, where these trees remained purely domestic affairs. This custom is generally said to have spread to Europe from America, where a large illuminated tree was set up in a public place at Pasadena in California in 1909. From here, the custom spread all over America, and then throughout the Christian world. Nowadays most towns all over Britain have public Christmas trees, decorated with coloured lights. These are often the focus of a large open-air carol service, and have anonymous gifts placed beneath them for hospitals, orphanages and charities. The largest and best-known of these public trees is the great fir put up each year in Trafalgar Square, beside Nelson's Column. Since 1947, this has been an annual gift from the people of Oslo to the people of London, to mark the Allied victory in the last war.

The eating of turkey has been popular ever since the turkey was first introduced to this country by way of France in the 16th century. It was the American Indians who first ate turkey, and this was the bird which the early American settlers ate on their first Thanksgiving Day, a custom which Americans have repeated ever since, and one which many historians believe played a certain part in influencing our own Christmas custom.

Before turkey, the traditional Christmas dish was boar's head, and the origin of this custom goes back to pagan times, when the boar's head was a sacred dish in many parts of northern Europe. In medieval times, those unable to afford the luxury of a boar's head usually feasted on goose (which still remains a great favourite at this time of year, especially in Europe). The eating of mince pies at Christmas has been customary since Elizabethan times, though the addition of Christmas Pudding to the menu came a century or two later. Christmas Pudding, originally called 'Plum Pudding', has a decidedly mixed history. In earlier times, the main ingredients of plum pudding included all kinds of rich food besides the traditional plums (usually in the form of prunes), raisins and mixed spices. In poorer families, where meat was a rarity, minced meat and offal were often included amongst the ingredients – the dish being a species of sweet, rich, hotch-potch haggis that would probably turn the stomach of all but the hearty yeomen who ate it!

In Scotland, until fairly recently Christmas was not the high point of the midwinter celebrations; these were reserved for Hogmanay (New Year). Indeed, until Victorian times this was so over most of England too. Much of what we now consider the Christmas atmosphere is in fact a German influence largely popularised by the works of Charles Dickens. Even in his famous *Christmas Carol*, Scrooge is considered merely misanthropic, rather than outrageous, in insisting that his workers stay at their office desks during Christmas Day – until his miraculous conversion, that is.

One can only imagine what Scrooge would have thought of our modern custom of holding office Christmas parties. These have only become universal over the past few decades, and now seem to incorporate many of the elements of the old Mischief Nights. The office party usually marks the end of business for the entire year, with the increasing practice being for most people to take the entire holiday between Christmas and New Year for the purpose of visiting the family or close relatives.

Many people nowadays make the excuse that they only celebrate Christmas 'for the children', yet despite falling church attendance the traditional Midnight Mass on Christmas Eve is still the most highly attended church service, along with the Easter Sunday Service. Christmas remains the season of good will towards all men, yet for some it is also the most lonely. Though it hardly qualifies as a tradition it is a chilling thought that enough people commit suicide at this time of year to fill any normal parish church.

The day after Christmas is St Stephen's Day, more popularly known as **Boxing Day**. This name derives from the custom of servants and tradespeople going round the houses on this day taking collections for their Christmas box, much as dustmen and postmen still do. In many villages there was also a custom called 'Stephening', which involved the vicar in providing a meal of bread, cheese and ale to his poorer parishioners. However this custom was eventually stopped when an increasing number of poor folk came to look upon it as their right to have a drunken jamboree at the vicar's expense, even going so far as to storm the vicarage when he refused to provide it!

The biggest day of the year for most Scotsmen is **New Year's Eve**, when Scots from all over Britain return home to celebrate Hogmanay. The name 'Hogmanay' is said to derive from a special cake which was baked for the occasion, though it almost certainly has some more ancient dialect origin which has since been forgotten. Nowadays the 'letting in' of the New Year at Hogmanay tends to involve parties with bagpipes and the dancing of traditional reels. These activities are usually accompanied by prodigious consumption of a local spirit known in Gaelic as *uisgebeatha*, which means 'water of life', though presumably for convenience and speed of ordering this is now more usually shortened to *uisge* (or sometimes, just plain 'Scotch'). Another prevalent custom in these parts is First Footing, which was described along with other New Year's customs at the start of this section.

All over the country it is customary to hold New Year's Eve parties, where on the stroke of midnight everyone joins hands and sings 'Auld Lang Syne', a traditional song taken from a poem by the great 18th-century Scots poet 'Rabbie' Burns. Another increasingly popular tradition is the celebration which takes place in Trafalgar Square in London, when tens of thousands of young people gather in festive mood to bring in the New Year – usually to the accompaniment of high-spirited dancing in the freezing waters of the fountains. A truly commendable, if somewhat perverse, example of our country's diligent observance of its customs!

More Traditional Recipes

For sources, see p. 94

Haggis

Many good butchers in England sell haggis. For the authentic taste of Scotland, but without the journey, simmer the haggis gently in water for 1 hr. Serve it with mashed neeps (turnips). And don't forget the glass of whisky to wash it down.

Sheep's offal (as below)
1/2lb (250g) mutton suet
1lb (500g) pinhead oatmeal
3 onions

Wash the stomach bag of a sheep perfectly clean, and turn it outside in. Scald and scrape it with a knife, then steep it in salted water until it is required.

Parboil the heart, lights and liver of the sheep. Grate the liver. Mince the other parts with the mutton suet. Toast the pinhead oatmeal in the oven. Parboil the onions. Chop them and add them with the oatmeal to the other ingredients. Season with salt and pepper. Fill the bag and add a little of the onion water.

Sew up the bag, leaving enough room for the oatmeal to swell. Prick the bag all over to prevent bursting. Put it on an enamel plate in a saucepan with enough boiling water to cover. Boil for 4 or 5 hrs, keeping the haggis constantly covered with water.

Bannocks

Scotland delights in a wide range of delicious and filling cakes, biscuits and breads, sweet and savoury. Bannocks are usually made from oatmeal and buttermilk. The Selkirk bannock is, oddly, quite different – a fruit loaf more like a lardy cake or the Welsh *bara brith*.

1 egg, beaten
1 pint (60cl) milk or buttermilk
1/4 tsp bicarbonate of soda
1/4 tsp salt
oatmeal

Stir the milk into the egg. Mix in the soda, salt and enough oatmeal to make a dropping batter.

Rub a girdle with a piece of suet. Pour the batter onto the girdle in small circles, as for drop scones. Cook them over a moderate heat until bubbles form on the top, then turn and cook on the other side.

Serve immediately. Delicious with butter and marmalade.

Yorkshire Pudding

The recipe for Yorkshire Pudding was first published in 1737, and arguments have raged ever since about the authentic way of cooking it. Certainly, it is delicious baked under a juicy joint of beef, offering the impossible choice between the crispy bits and the beefy bits. Do not forget, however, that with the addition of a handful of sage, parsley and thyme it enhances roast pork. And if you have any room left after that, why not try eating it with butter and sugar, or with golden syrup – another traditional favourite.

4 oz (125g) flour
pinch of salt
1 egg
1/2 pint milk

Mix the flour and salt, make a well in the centre and break in the egg. Add a little milk. Beginning at the centre, stir the ingredients into a batter, gradually pouring in the remaining milk.

40 min before the joint is cooked, pour the pudding into a roasting tin, under the rack on which the joint is cooking.

Saffron Cake

One of the most costly spices in early English cooking is saffron. Today it survives only in yeast cakes and buns, like this Cornish native. Try saffron cake with lashings of real clotted cream for an authentic taste of the West Country.

1lb (500g) plain flour
1 oz (30g) dried yeast
pinch of salt
8 oz (250g) butter
4 oz (125g) sugar
8 oz (250g) mixed fruit
and chopped peel
2 tsp saffron infused
in 4 tbsp boiling water
warm milk

Mix together the flour, yeast and salt. Rub in the butter, Stir in the sugar and fruit. Mix to a dough with the saffron liquid and sufficient milk. Leave to rise for 2 hrs in a warm place.

Divide the mixture into two tins. Leave for a further hr, then bake in a preheated oven 180°C (350°F or Mark 4) for 1 hr or until golden.

Steak and Kidney Pie

This is the best of all the savoury pies. To celebrate the delights of the English kitchen, why not add 2 hardboiled free-range eggs, quartered, and 9 fresh oysters (when there's an 'R' in the month, of course)?

1 lb (500g) stewing steak, cubed
4 oz (125g) kidney, cubed
flour
salt and pepper
8 oz (250g) flaky pastry

Roll the meat in seasoned flour, place it in a casserole with water to cover, and stew gently for 1½-2 hrs.

When the meat is cool, put it in a pie dish and cover it with the pastry. Make a hole in the middle and lay on any pastry decorations you wish. Brush with beaten egg or milk. Bake in a preheated oven 220°C (425°F or Mark 7) for 30 min.

Apple Pie

The English apple pie is usually made from cooking apples, stewed in sugar under a pastry crust. This 18th-c. recipe from Bedfordshire is traditionally eaten at Christmas.

4 large cooking apples,
peeled and cored
3 tbsp demerara sugar
1 tsp grated lemon peel
1 lb (500g) shortcrust pastry
1 pint (60cl) pale ale
¼ tsp grated nutmeg
pinch of cinnamon
3 cloves

Place the apples in a deep, buttered dish. Sprinkle with 2 tbsp of sugar and the lemon peel. Cover with a thick pastry crust and bake in a preheated oven 230°C (450°F or Mark 8) for 30 min.

Lift off the pastry. Heat together all the remaining ingredients (do not boil) and pour the liquid over the apples. Cut the pastry into 4, and place one piece on each apple. Serve very hot in bowls.

Mrs Beeton's Hot Punch

'Punch is a beverage made of various spirituous liquors or wine, hot water, the acid juice of fruits, and sugar. It is considered to be very intoxicating; but this is probably because the spirit being partly sheathed by the mucilaginous juice and the sugar, its strength does not appear to the taste so great as it really is.'

½ pint (30cl) rum
½ pint (30cl) brandy
4 oz (125g) sugar (use cubes)
1 large lemon
½ tsp grated nutmeg
1 pint (60cl) boiling water

Rub the sugar all over the lemon until it has absorbed all the zest. Put the sugar in a punch bowl and add the strained juice of the lemon. Pour over the water, and stir well. Add the rum, brandy and nutmeg and mix well. All ingredients must be thoroughly mixed together.

Country Customs & Town Traditions
A Regional Guide

Maypole dancing at Abinger Fair

*Entries marked with an asterisk are either specifically mentioned in the preceding Seasonal Section or are associated with customs described there. (For precise page references see Index.) When not otherwise stated, further details of all these events can be obtained from the local Tourist Board or Tourist Information Centre. In the case of festivals, write to the Festival Director of the appropriate town or city for a programme of events (see Useful Addresses, p. 95).

London

Daily **Ceremony of the Keys**
Tower of London EC3
The world's oldest military ceremony. Every night the Chief Warder in beefeater costume sets off at 9.40, accompanied by an escort of the Brigade of Guards, to lock up the main towers and West Gate. The escort carrying the keys is given the traditional challenge, 'Whose keys?' to which he replies, 'Queen Elizabeth's keys'. *Write to the Governor of the Tower for permission to attend*

Daily **Changing of the Guard**
Buckingham Palace SW1
The Queen's London residence, Buckingham Palace, is guarded by the Queen's Guard – which includes the Coldstream Guards, the oldest serving regiment in the British Army (and possibly the world). Each morning from Monday until Saturday at 11 this Guard is ceremonially changed, and the Keys to the Palace symbolically handed over, inside the railings in front of the Palace. It's a traditional pageant of great pomp, with a military band playing. In summer it attracts huge crowds of tourists, though even then you can always get a good view of the Guards marching to and from Chelsea of Westminster Barracks.

Daily **Changing of the Horse Guards**
Horse Guards Arch, Whitehall W1
Every morning at 10.30 (10 on Sundays) the splendidly attired Queen's mounted Life Guards with their shining armour and plumed helmets leave Hyde Park Barracks. From here they proceed down the Mall to parade at Horse Guards in Whitehall, where the Changing of the Guard ceremony takes place inside the forecourt. A little less crowded and more intimate than the ceremony at the Palace.

Jan-Mar **Chinese New Year**
Gerrard Street, Soho W1
The big annual celebration for Britain's Chinese community in the midst of London's Chinatown. The streets and shops are hung with traditional Chinese decorations and there's a colourful procession of huge paper tigers, lanterns and fearsome dragons. Interesting novelty badges depicting the Year of the Rabbit, Year of the Snake, etc. Takes place on Sunday morning. *Ask in your local Chinese restaurant for the precise date, which varies*

Feb 6 **Anniversary of Queen Elizabeth II's Accession**
Hyde Park
A traditional 41-gun salute is fired at 12 noon by the King's Troop of the Royal Horse Artillery outside Wellington Barracks. (An alternative salute is also fired at the Tower of London at 1 pm by the Honourable Artillery Company.) Other royal dates on which salutes are fired include the Queen's Birthday (Apr 21), Prince Philip's Birthday (Jun 2), the Queen's Official Birthday (2nd Sat in Jun), and the Queen Mother's Birthday (Aug 4).

Shrove Tuesday **JIF National Pancake Race and Pancake Greeze**
Lincoln's Inn Fields WC2 and Westminster School SW1

Traditional pancake race (now sponsored by lemon juice firm) with several celebrity and restaurateur entries, attracting large jolly Fleet St and City crowd. Less well-known is the Westminster School 'Greeze', a traditional bunfight in which scholars fight for pieces of a giant pancake made out of candlewax and horsehair or a similar obnoxious mix! The winner – the one with the largest piece – receives a golden guinea from the Headmaster. *For permission to attend apply well beforehand in writing to the Headmaster*

Sat in Mar or Apr **Oxford and Cambridge Boat Race**
River Thames, Putney to Mortlake

The world's most famous 'boat race', in which the two coxed eights row it out over the traditional 4-mile course. Crowds line the route wearing dark or light blue rosettes to cheer on their favourites. Try watching from a riverside pub by Hammersmith Bridge. Race starts according to the tide.

Maundy Thursday **Royal Maundy Money**
Westminster Abbey/other major church

On the Thursday before Good Friday the Queen attends this centuries-old ceremony. Until the reign of James II it was customary for the monarch to wash the feet of as many poor people as there were years of his reign. Nowadays the Queen distributes Maundy Money to as many of the poor as there are years of her reign. These specially minted coins are highly sought-after by collectors.

Easter Sunday **Easter Parade and Fair**
Battersea Park and Hampstead Heath

The parade takes place on the morning of Easter Sunday and consists of a carnival procession of ladies wearing Easter bonnets (which range from the spectacular to the hilarious) preceded by a parade of 'old crocks' and vintage vehicles. In the afternoon there's all the fun of the fair on Hampstead Heath, and afterwards a chance for a pint 'down at the Old Bull and Bush', which features in the traditional Cockney song.

May 29 **Oak Apple Day**
Royal Hospital, Chelsea SW3

Celebrations to mark the Restoration of Charles II in 1660, who later founded the Royal Hospital, home of the celebrated 'Chelsea Pensioners'. On Oak Apple Day, the Pensioners in their famous red topcoats have a special march-past, all wearing their medals and a sprig of oak (to commemorate Charles's escape from the Roundheads by hiding in an oak tree).

May-Jul **Royal Academy Summer Exhibition**
Burlington House, Piccadilly W1

The Royal Academy's celebrated 'Summer Exhibition', which includes paintings submitted by artists from all over the country. The opening in May is one of the events of the social season, with society photographers vying for 'interesting' photos of 'Deb' types and aristocratic matrons against the background of the exhibits – which range through a wide variety of mainstream art by amateurs and professionals alike.

Ascension Day, May 24 **Beating the Bounds**
Starts Chapel Royal, Tower of London EC3

A ceremony dating from medieval times. The Chief Yeoman Warder of the Tower leads a procession of choirboys carrying canes around the parish boundaries. The choirboys beat each of the 31 boundary stones in the surrounding streets.

Sat nearest Jun 11 **Trooping the Colour**
Horse Guards Parade, Whitehall W1

London's most spectacular military parade. The celebration of the Queen's

Official Birthday is marked by a parade of the assembled Brigade of Guards. This 2-hr pageant has its origins in the 17th c., when the colours were paraded before each man in the regiment so that he could recognise them in battle. The intricate march-past includes the massed bands of five regiments, and is acknowledged by Her Majesty the Queen on horseback, usually accompanied by the Duke of Edinburgh and Prince Charles. The ceremony is witnessed by large crowds from the tiered stands which are erected specially for the occasion around Horse Guards Parade. *Apply between Jan-Mar to HQ Household Division, Horse Guards, Whitehall, London SW1*

1st 3 weeks in Jul City of London Festival

The City welcomes visitors into its many ancient churches and buildings during this festival. In addition to major concerts, you'll find office workers enjoying the lunchtime street theatre and many other light-hearted fringe events.

3rd week in Jul Swan Upping

Temple Steps, Embankment SW3
Each year the Royal Keeper of the Swans and his crew set off to count all the swans on the River Thames. By tradition these swans belong to the Queen and certain City livery companies, and all have to be 'marked' with their owner's symbol. The boatmen go as far upstream as Henley.

Late Jul Doggett's Coat and Badge Race

London Bridge to Chelsea
This traditional single-scull race for Thames Watermen dates from 1715, making it one of the oldest boat races in the world. Each year the winner receives a scarlet coat and silver badge, the first of which was presented by the actor Thomas Doggett. Fine examples of these winners' coats and badges can be seen at the Greenwich Naval Museum.

Late Jul-Sep Promenade Concerts

Royal Albert Hall SW7
This summer season of concerts was founded by Sir Henry Wood in 1895 with the idea of bringing classical music within popular range. Low price 'Promenade' tickets available for areas without seats if you queue on the night. Enthusiastic – and mostly young – devotees enjoy the complete range from *avant-garde* to pre-classical. Tickets by ballot for the traditional revelries of the 'Last Night of the Proms'. *Apply Box Office 01-589 8212*

Aug Bank Hol Weekend Notting Hill Carnival

Notting Hill W11
Colourful carnival involving floats of steel bands followed by revellers and dancers. An informal community event which has evolved into London's greatest street festival. It is to be hoped that the unfortunate violence of previous years is now a thing of the past. Our answer to the famous Rio Carnival.

*1st Sun in Oct Costermongers' Harvest Festival

St Martin's in the Fields, Trafalgar Square WC2
London's own Harvest Festival, attended by the famous Cockney 'Pearly Kings and Queens' all dressed in their traditional sequined regalia. Each 'monarch' brings fruit, flowers and vegetables and afterwards they have a colourful get-together and jamboree.

1st Sun in Nov London to Brighton Veteran Car Race

Starts Hyde Park Corner SW1
Each year scores of 'old crocks' and vintage contraptions of all kinds set off amidst bangs and clouds of smoke for the 60-mile journey. Drivers and passengers, braving the elements in period costumes and bonnets, grit their teeth and wave bravely as they depart on the bone-shaking journey.

Beating the Bounds at the Tower of London

Changing the Guard at Buckingham Palace
Opposite: The Queen's Bodyguard of Yeomen of the Guard at St James's Palace

63

Lord Mayor's Show

2nd Sat in Nov Lord Mayor's Show
Guildhall EC2 to Law Courts WC2
London's best traditional free show,
when the newly-elected Lord Mayor of
London drives in his state coach with a
colourful procession to take his oath
from the Lord Chief Justice. Bells ring
and cheering crowds line the route.
For the rest of the year the Lord
Mayor's coach is on display at the
London Museum.

**★*Early Nov* State Opening of
Parliament**
Houses of Parliament SW1
Traditional opening of Parliament
after the summer recess. The Queen
drives in the Irish State Coach from
Buckingham Palace to deliver her
speech (which outlines the Govern-
ment's policy for the coming session).
The speech is delivered in the House
of Lords to members of both houses. A
royal salute is fired in St James's Park.

**★*New Year's Eve* Bringing in the New
Year**
Trafalgar Square WC2
High jinks and general jollity to mark
the year's end. Thousands of young
people in festive mood take over the
square, with capering figures 'cooling
off' in the freezing waters of the
fountains. Even attendant 'bobbies'
occasionally join in the fun.

South-East

★*Jan 31* Dicing for Old Maid's Money
Guildford, Surrey
Curious charity tradition dating from
17th c. One Jack Haw asked that the
Mayor choose two poor serving maids
and let them play dice for money from
his annuity. Several years later a
certain John Parson left a sum of
money which is now paid to the loser!

★*1st week in May* Guildford Fair
Guildford, Surrey
Week-long annual city fair which
includes a wide variety of cultural
events and entertainments. The major
event here is the Pageant of Guildford
which features re-enactments of
events from the city's history – often
including a Civil War encounter
between Roundheads and Cavaliers in
full costume with pikes and staves.

**★*4th week in May-1st week in Aug*
Glyndebourne Festival Opera**
Glyndebourne, Ringmer, Sussex
World-famous season of opera at
Glyndebourne, with its celebrated lake
and gardens (where you can take a
summer evening picnic in idyllic
surroundings between the acts).
Performers of international standing in
first-class productions.
See *Festivals*, p. 94

3rd week in May **Mayoring Day**
Rye, Sussex

In earlier centuries this ancient Cinque Port (now over 2 miles inland) was allowed to mint its own coinage. This is now commemorated on the day the new Mayor is elected, when he appears on the balcony of *The George Hotel* and throws 'hot' pennies down to the children in the street below.

Jul 19 **Little Edith's Treat**
Piddinghoe, Sussex

A village celebration deriving from the death, over a century ago, of a three-month-old child. When Edith Croft died in 1868, her grandmother directed that each year on the anniversary of Edith's birthday £100 should be spent. Now there is a church service, a village fête and races.

3rd & 4th week in Jul **Chichester Festivities**
Chichester, Sussex

All kinds of activities and entertainments, including large-scale cultural festival which is specially known for its excellent theatre productions. Once every three years the Southern Cathedrals Festival is held here at this time. (On the other two years it alternates between Winchester and Salisbury.)
See *Festivals*, p. 94

1st Sat in Aug **National Town Criers' Championship**
Hastings, Sussex

Competitors from all over the land, carrying their hand bells and wearing their full ceremonial regalia, converge annually for a vocal Battle of Hastings. To begin with, there's a procession from the Town Hall, with the Hastings and St Leonards Band and the Mayor and his corporation. The contest is judged on power of voice and smartness of appearance. After a fanfare of trumpets, the competitors are rowed out to a small island over 50 yards from the spectators. From here they bellow the traditional 'Oyez! Oyez!' and read out a 150-word standard proclamation to the assembled judges and crowds across the water. The winner receives a splendid Challenge Cup and a sum of money (donated by a Sunday newspaper – not, as one might expect, a throat lozenge manufacturer).

Mid Aug **The Venetian Festival**
Hythe, Sussex

Celebration marking something which never happened – Napoleon's invasion in 1805. This celebration, which takes place biennially in even-numbered years, first started in 1854. A night procession of illuminated floats depicting local, historic and humorous incidents moves down the tree-lined Royal Military Canal, followed by a firework display.

Sep **Apron and Clog Race**
Kew, Surrey

A 60-year-old race for students who work for, or are attached to, the Royal Botanical Gardens at Kew.
Competitors wear special clogs and aprons and race through the gardens for a prize of a bottle of wine and the chance of immortality by having a plant species named after them.

*Nov 5 **Bonfire Night Celebrations**
Lewes, Sussex

The most spectacular Guy Fawkes celebrations in southern England. A torchlight procession in fancy dress is organised by the local bonfire societies, and besides the traditional burning of the Guy other effigies of those they love to hate are placed on the fire. A festive night ending in fireworks and customary merriment around the fire.

Dec 24 **Hoodening**
Folkestone, Kent

A local Christmas Eve celebration involving a traditional effigy of a horse. The Hooden Horse (which has the skull of a real horse) is taken in procession from house to house with carol singing and much revelry, accompanied by musicians and traditional characters in fancy dress.

South

Mar 25 **The Tichbourne Dole**
Tichbourne, Hampshire
One of Britain's most celebrated, and certainly one of its strangest customs. When Lady Marabella Tichbourne was on her deathbed 800 years ago, she begged her husband to give some land to the poor villagers of Tichbourne. Her husband seized a large faggot from the fire and declared that he would give as much land as she could circle before the faggot burnt out. Whereupon, the dying lady rose from her bed and crawled on a journey that circumscribed no less than 23 acres. As she lay dying, Lady Marabella swore to her husband that if ever her sacred gift was not fulfilled the Tichbourne name would die out in a generation consisting of seven daughters. This land, known to this day as The Crawls, still yields one and a half tons of flour for the villagers, which is shared out each year. There has only been one break in this custom, when Sir Henry Tichbourne decided in 1799 that the flour should be given to the church instead. After this, the next inheritor of the title had seven daughters, and immediately the dole was restored!

Shrove Tuesday **Olney Pancake Race**
Olney, Buckinghamshire
The oldest pancake race in the country, dating from 1485. The race attracts large crowds and is heralded by the ancient Olney Pancake Bell. The competing housewives tear down a special 415-yard course in the High Street with their frying pans. The strictly observed rules decree that the contestants must wear headscarves and toss the pancakes three times on their journey. The first lady to serve her pancake to the bellringer standing at the church door is given a kiss and declared the Pancake Champion.

May 1 **May Morning Celebrations**
Magdalen College, Oxford
As the sun rises on May Day the choristers of Magdalen College assemble on the top of the 144ft Magdalen Tower and sing a Latin hymn, *'Te Deum Patrem Colimus'*, locally known as the 'May Song'. A large crowd gathers beneath the Tower, and as soon as the College Bell rings at the end of the hymn, Morris dancers disperse to dance at certain spots throughout the city.

May **Weighing-in Ceremony**
High Wycombe, Buckinghamshire
A curious 18th-c. custom which takes place after the election of the new Mayor and Mayoress. The Chief Inspector of Weights and Measures weighs the new Mayor and Mayoress, as well as the ex-Mayor and ex-Mayoress. The town Beadle then rings his bell, and calls out 'Oyez! Oyez!' and reads out their weights to the assembled company. The custom is thought to date from a time when there was a ban on over-corporate members of the corporation!

⋆Whit Monday **Morris Dancing**
Bampton, Oxfordshire
Some of the finest displays of Morris dancing in the land by the celebrated Bampton Morris Dancers. Traditional dancing with garlands and accordion goes on throughout the day in the streets and gardens of this picturesque West Oxfordshire village.

May 29 **Grovely Rights Procession**
Wishford Magna, Wiltshire
Remnant of an ancient May Day custom which centuries ago became amalgamated with a protest over village rights, and is now celebrated on Oak Apple Day. In the morning the villagers exercise their right to collect 'all kinde of deade snapping woode Boughes and Sticks' from the local Grovely wood and then proceed by coach to Salisbury, where they march in procession to the cathedral calling out and carrying banners proclaiming 'Grovely! Grovely! And all Grovely!'

⋆Jun 23 **Summer Solstice Ceremony**
Stonehenge, Avebury, Wiltshire
The revival of a custom which is probably all of 4000 years old. The

Olney Pancake Race

Most Ancient Order of Druids holds a ceremony at sunrise as the tip of the sun peeps above the Heel Stone of Stonehenge – though why they have switched this from Midsummer Morning to a later day remains unclear. Attracts large crowds of mainly young people from all over the country and abroad.

Sun after Jun 4 Wall Pulpit Sermon
Magdalen College, Oxford

This 500-year-old ceremony is said to date from the time when there was a hospital on the site of the college. A sermon is delivered from the stone pulpit which is set in the wall of the first quadrangle of the college.

2nd Mon in Jun Garter Ceremony
Windsor, Berkshire

The Order of the Garter is bestowed by the reigning monarch, and has been since the 14th c. This is the highest order of chivalry in the land. The Knights of the Order, together with the Queen, attend the special service in St George's Chapel, dressed in their traditional costume of cloaks, plumed hats and garters. After the service the Knights of the Order file out and there is a procession with the Household Cavalry.

End of Jul The Battle of Flowers
Jersey, Channel Islands

This event is renowned as Europe's greatest floral carnival. It originated in 1902 as part of the local coronation celebrations for King Edward VII. The main event is the procession, which contains many floral exhibits of astonishing originality and beauty – such as windmills with turning floral sails, engines and life-sized animals. There are also intricate floral tableaux depicting events from the island's history. The high point of the procession is the appearance of Miss Jersey on her floral carriage. At the end of the grand floral procession, a signal is given and the Battle of Flowers begins.

Aug 1 **Knighthood of the Old Green**
Southampton, Hampshire
A ceremonial game of bowls on what is said to be the oldest bowling green in the world. The competitors (called 'gentlemen commoners') dress in top hats and tails and are supervised by 'Knights in Green'. This competition has been held since 1776, though the green itself is several centuries older.

Mon & Tue after first Sun in Sep
St Giles' Fair
St Giles, Oxford
One of the largest and oldest street fairs in England. It still occupies its original site on Magdalen Street and St Giles, and has taken place, with only a few breaks, since the 11th c. In medieval times it was a produce fair for the surrounding countryside though now it is largely a funfair.

Oct 7 **Bell-ringers' Feast**
Twyford, Hampshire
When returning home late on the night of Apr 22 1754, a local landowner called William Davis lost his way in the fog. On hearing the bells of Twyford Church ringing in the distance he changed direction, and thus avoided falling to his death in a deep chalk pit. In his will he left £1 to the local bell-ringers, to be paid on Oct 7, on condition thay they rang the bells on the morning and evenings of that day. Afterwards, the bell-ringers celebrate with a traditional feast (which nowadays costs rather more than £1!).

Oct 21 **Trafalgar Day Ceremony**
Portsmouth, Hampshire
A commemoration of Britain's greatest naval hero at the home of the British Navy. A service is held aboard Nelson's flagship HMS *Victory*, during which a wreath is laid on the exact spot where he fell in 1805 – when he is said to have uttered those famous last words 'Kiss me, Hardy'. (Claimed by some stalwart naval buffs to have been a mishearing of 'Kismet [i.e. Fate], Hardy'.)

Sat nearest Nov 30 **Eton Wall Game**
Eton, Buckinghamshire
This unique traditional football game, whose rules baffle all but the participants, is played annually along a narrow field bordered by an ancient wall. One team consists of Collegers (the scholars who live inside the College) and the other of Oppidans (the rest of the pupils, who live outside the College). Amidst much cheering the aristocratic lads scrimmage and cover themselves in mud – largely to no avail, however. A goal is usually scored here once a century. In 1909 one was scored after 46 goalless years, amidst scenes of unbridled celebration and astonishment.

★Dec 26 **St Albans' Mummers**
St Albans, Hertfordshire
The ancient practice of mumming eventually evolved into the traditional Mumming Plays, only a few of which survive over the whole country. Here the mumming is practised in its original form as a Christmas custom. A group of men wearing womens' clothes, and vice versa, go on a round of the houses bringing Christmas cheer, playing japes and generally making merry.

West Country

★Jan 16 **Wassailing the Apple Trees**
Norton Fitzwarren, Somerset
Custom dating back at least to Saxon times, and taking place on the original Twelfth Night (according to pre-1752 calendar). The Wassail Queen is carried through the orchard and pours a libation from the Wassail Cup into the fork of each tree. Firing of shotguns and singing of traditional songs, preceded and followed by drinking of mulled punch.

★May 1 **Hobby Horse Festival**
Padstow, Cornwall
May Day celebrations with much rural jollity, including the celebrated 'Obby Oss' which frolics about the town. Proceedings start in the morning at 11

outside the Golden Lion Inn, where the 'Obby Oss' is stabled. According to local legend the original custom was thought to protect the town from invaders.

May 1 Cheese Rolling
Randwick, Gloucester
Time-honoured custom whose exact significance is uncertain, involving three large cheeses adorned with garlands. These are carried in procession to the church graveyard, where they are ceremonially rolled three times each around the walls of the church. Afterwards the cheeses are carried back to the village green where they are sliced into pieces and divided amongst the parishioners. There's also cheese-rolling at nearby Birdlip, where the cheeses are rolled down a hillside and raced.

*May 8 Furry Dance
Helston, Cornwall
This is the famous dance which features in the popular traditional song 'All together in the floral dance . . . ' ('Furry' means 'floral' in lapsed local dialect.) The revels reach a climax at noon as the Guildhall clock strikes. The dancers wear flowers and proceed in and out of the open doorways of the houses. Also the 'Hal-an-Tow', a form of traditional May Day mumming play.

4th week in May–1st week in Jun Bath Festival
Bath, Avon
Bath is renowned for its Roman Bath and its Georgian architecture. The International Festival of Music today holds concerts and performances in many of these lovely buildings. There are also a wide range of exhibitions and fringe events.
See *Festivals*, p. 94

Mid-May Competitive Festival of Music, Speech, Drama and Dancing
Cheltenham, Gloucester
One of several festivals which have established Cheltenham as the arts centre of the West. There's also an International Music Festival (2nd &

3rd weeks in Jul) at which original commissioned works are given first performances, and a Festival of Literature (mid-Oct) at which novelists, poets and critics discuss literary matters and award prizes.
See *Festivals*, p. 94

*Tues late in Jul Lammas Fair
Exeter, Devon
A Lammas-tide fair originating from Saxon times. Before the fair begins there is the celebrated 'Displaying the Glove' ceremony, which dates from a charter granted by Edward I in the 13th c. A white stuffed glove is carried through the streets and the famous proclamation is read out, which declares: 'Oyez! Oyez! The glove is up, the fair has begun, no man shall be arrested until the glove is taken down. God bless the Queen!'

3rd Sun in Jul Tolpuddle Martyrs Procession
Tolpuddle, Dorset
A commemoration of the famous Tolpuddle Martyrs, six agricultural labourers who formed themselves into a trade union in 1834 and were sentenced to be 'transported beyond the seas' (to the penal colony in Australia). A procession organised by the National Union of Farm Workers marking an event which once split the country and played a pioneering role in the formation of the modern trade union movement.

*Aug 24 Blessing the Mead
Gulval, Cornwall
The annual St Bartholomew's Day ceremony of Blessing the Mead, the ancient Cornish beverage made from fermented honey which in medieval times was our national drink. St Bartholomew is the patron saint of beekeepers, and his blessing is called upon by no less a personage than 'The Alderman of the Fraternity of St Bartholomew of the Craft of Mystery of Free Meadmakers of Great Britain and Northern Ireland'. Ample opportunity to sample this interesting drink.

Last week in Aug **Three Choirs Festival**
Gloucester (in 1983)
The Three Choirs Festival, believed to be Europe's oldest continuous music festival, was founded over 250 years ago, and it is a showcase for choral, orchestral and chamber music. It rotates between the cathedral cities of Hereford, Gloucester and Worcester. See *Festivals*, p. 94

*Last Thur in Oct **Punkie Night**
Hinton St George, Somerset
An ancient Hallowe'en celebration dating in this village from an obscure incident which is said to have taken place in medieval times. 'Punkies' are hollowed-out pumpkins with faces carved into them and lighted candles placed inside, which the children taken from house to house begging for candles. It is considered bad luck to turn away the children empty-handed. Afterwards there is a procession round the village boundaries.

*Nov 5 **Tar-Barrel Rolling**
Ottery St Mary, Devon
November 5th celebrations with a difference. Nine barrels of tar are set alight, and then participants see how far they can run carrying them on their backs with the flames trailing out behind them. Finally the barrels are rolled down the street and a traditional bonfire is lit to burn the Guy.

Wed after Nov 5 **Hatherleigh Fire Festival**
Hatherleigh, Devon
An all-day carnival culminating in lighted barrels being carried on a sledge through the town accompanied by the local jazz band. These celebrations derive from ancient Celtic lore when fires were lit on top of the hills to protect the villagers from the spirits of the dead who roamed about at this time of year.

Fri in Nov **Court Lees**
Wareham, Dorset
A custom dating from Norman times, when the Lees was set up to weigh the local loaves, inspect the chimneys and taste the ale to see if it was up to standard. In the week preceding the Lees the Bailiff and his officers tour the pubs and hotels stalwartly doing their duty. The Lees is held in the Town Hall, when these matters are discussed, along with grazing rights.

Before Christmas **Cutting the Glastonbury Thorn**
Glastonbury, Somerset
The ancient, though largely apocryphal Christian legends associated with the Glastonbury Thorn make it one of the most celebrated trees in Christendom. According to superstition the tree always flowers on the Christmas Day of the old calendar, and for centuries now a sprig has been cut from the tree by the vicar of the Church of St John the Baptist to be sent to adorn the Christmas dinner table of the reigning monarch. Traditional performances of the Miracles of Glastonbury are enacted in the ruins of the ancient Abbey (Jul and Sep).

East Anglia

Early Jan **Cakes & Ale Ceremony**
Bury St Edmunds, Suffolk
A service is held at St Mary's Church in memory of the town's benefactor, Jankyn Smith, who died in 1480. Afterwards a celebration is held at the Guildhall where cakes are served with sherry (which substitutes for the ale).

Feb 2 **Carlow's Charity**
Woodbridge, Suffolk
Carlow's Charity, sometimes known as 'the Bread Dole', was founded by George Carlow who died in 1738. In his will he left instructions that the rent from his property should be used to maintain his tomb and that £1 worth of bread should be bought from the town's two poorest bakers for distribution to the needy. Each year the bread is distributed by the rector, the verger and two churchwardens to selected villagers.

*Shrove Tuesday Pancake Races
Ely, Cambridgeshire
A traditional pancake race through the streets of Ely. Highly popular event in which local celebrities compete with the current Miss Anglia.

4th Wed in Mar National Heavy Horse Show
Alwalton, Cambridgeshire
The national show for dray and shire horses, once the backbone of our nation's agriculture and, on occasions, transport into battle for heavily armoured knights. Fine examples of several breeds, some still used for ploughing and occasional carting duties. A rare chance to see a rapidly vanishing sight.

*Whit Monday The Dunmow Flitch
Great Dunmow, Essex
This world-famous custom is now held irregularly, though it has lasted since the 13th c. and is mentioned in the works of Chaucer. The main proceedings consists of a 'trial', before a local jury of bachelors and spinsters, in which married couples compete for a flitch (side) of bacon. The winners are the couple who can persuade the jury, in the face of searching questions, that they haven't argued or wished themselves single at any time throughout the previous year. Intrepid participants must have been married for at least a year and a day.

Whit Tuesday Dicing for Bibles
St Ives, Cambridgeshire
A custom going back to 1675, when a certain Dr Wilde decreed in his will that £10 each year must be spent on the purchase of Bibles. His instructions were that these should be given to six boys and girls said to be 'of good report'. At noon precisely, the Bibles are allocated to the children by casting dice.

2nd weekend in Jun Aldeburgh Festival
Aldeburgh, Suffolk
This small seaside town now hosts one of the world's most prestigious music festivals. The festival itself was originated by the composer Benjamin Britten, who used to live here, and through his influence the event began to attract international performers of the highest calibre. The main focus of the festival is the superbly renovated Snape Maltings which is capable of housing both chamber and orchestral concerts.

2nd week in Jun Merry-go-round Mayor
Southwold, Suffolk
The fair held here dates from a charter granted by Henry VII. The original charter was destroyed by fire and a new one was granted by William IV. This is read out on Trinity Monday at the start of the three-day fair by the Town Clerk. Then according to custom the fair is opened by the Mayor and the members of his corporation taking a ride on a roundabout. Afterwards watching children are given 3p each by the Mayor to spend at the fair.

Jul Rose Fair
Wisbech, Cambridgeshire
Despite its name, this is in fact a Strawberry Fair, and as such the greatest in the land. Throughout the week-long celebrations stalls attended by girls in period costume sell panniers of local strawberries. There is also a carnival with all the usual fairground entertainments.

Aug Lavender Harvest
Heacham, Norfolk
Lavender was introduced to this country neary 2000 years ago by the Romans, and has been grown in this area ever since. Norfolk Lavender at Caley Hill, Heacham, is the centre of this country's lavender industry, and each year in August the shrubs are harvested for the production of lavender water and other perfumes. A unique historic and aromatic experience.

Last Fri in Oct **Oyster Festival**
Colchester, Essex
By tradition, you can only eat oysters
when there's an 'R' in the month. This
ceremony marks the official opening of
the famous Colchester season. The
Mayor and his dignitaries leave in a
fishing boat to take part in the first
oyster dredge of the season, and on
return they are served the customary
refreshment of gin and gingerbread,
which they share with guests.

★Dec 24 **Festival of Nine Lessons
and Carols**
King's College Chapel, Cambridge
The annual Carol Service held by the
celebrated choir of King's College
amidst the splendours of the Chapel.
The best-known carol service in the
land – an experience which lives up to
all expectation. It has been broadcast
regularly since 1928, and the form of
the service is said to follow ancient
usage from the 6th-c. Byzantine
church. The high point is the solo
singing by a young chorister of the first
verse of 'Once in Royal David's City'.

Every Sat **John Sayer Charity**
Woodbridge, Suffolk
Another well-known Woodbridge
charity, similar to Carlow's Charity.
This one was instigated by John Sayer
who died in 1638. In his will he
decreed that the rent from 15 acres of
his land should be used to provide
bread for poor villagers. This was to be
handed out every Sunday, in
perpetuity. The day has now been
changed to Saturday to make sure that
the loaves are fresh.

Midlands

★Jan 6 **Haxey Hood Game**
Haxey, Lincolnshire
At the end of the 13th c., while Lady
de Mowbray was riding near Haxey,
her hood was blown off in the wind.
Immediately 13 local farm workers
gave chase to the hood and returned it
to her. Lady de Mowbray was so
touched by this chivalrous display that

in her will she left a piece of land to the
village, on condition that the event was
re-enacted each year. To this day, this
piece of land is known as the
'Hoodlands', and each year on Twelfth
Day Eve the villagers play a form of
no-rules rough-house football with the
'hood' as a ball. However, some
historians maintain that this game has
origins which long precede this
incident – stemming from an ancient
Celtic sacrifice game which was linked
with Twelfth Night celebrations.

Sun nearest Feb 2 **Cradle Rocking
Ceremony**
Blidworth, Nottinghamshire
This ancient ceremony re-enacting the
presentation of the infant Christ in the
Temple, once a regular feature of
medieval Miracle Plays, was revived by
the vicar of the Church of St Mary in
1922. The most recently baptised male
child in the parish is placed in a cradle
decorated with flowers, and during the
dedication service is ceremonially
rocked 12 times before being handed
back to his parents.

★Shrove Tuesday **Shrovetide Football**
Ashbourne, Derbyshire
A typical wild Shrovetide football
game with precious few rules, a sight
which was once familiar throughout
rural England. This game starts at 2pm
outside the Green Man Hotel and is
played between the village 'Up'ards'
and the 'Down'ards' (those living either
side of the Henmore stream). The
'pitch', over three miles long, includes
several muddy streams – the rest lives
up to all boisterous expectations!

Easter **Running Auction**
Bourne, Lincolnshire
When a local landowner called Robert
Clay died in 1770 he left a plot of land
called the 'White Bread Meadow' to be
auctioned annually for rent. The
proceeds were to be used to provide
bread for the poor people of the
Eastgate Ward, and this practice still
continues. During the curious auction,
bids are only valid in the time it takes
two boys to run up the road and back.

*Easter Monday Bottle Kicking & Hare Pie Scrambling
Hallaton, Leicestershire
A hugely popular event which started in 1771, though its precise origins remain in dispute. Amidst a carnival atmosphere the vicar leads the assembled villagers (complete with brass band) to a piece of land called Hare Pie Bank. Here a large hare pie is ritually divided and pieces are thrown to the crowds to be scrambled for. After this a game of bottle kicking takes place between the villagers of Hallaton and nearby Midbourne. The three 'bottles' (small wooden iron-hooped barrels which are filled with beer) are kicked by the mêlée of villagers with the aim of getting all of them across the respective boundaries of either village. Eventually, after much rough and tumble, the winners drink the contents of the bottles with due solemnity.

Last Thur in May **Wicken Love Feast**
Wicken, Northamptonshire
A typical village custom, which dates from the time when the rectories of Wickamon and Wickdive were united into one parish. A brief service is held at the parish church, and the vicar then leads a procession to the 'Gospel Elm' by the Old Rectory. Here the parishioners share a feast of cakes and ale (now usually wine).

*Last Sat in May Ickwell May Fair
Ickwell Green, Bedfordshire
One of the best May Day celebrations in the land, this one has been going since Elizabethan times. All the traditional events – including dancing round the maypole on the green, Morris dancers, and a May Queen. Also two special local characters, called 'Moggies' – men dressed as women with blackened faces and ragged clothes who take part in the procession.

*2nd half of May Well Dressing
Tissington, Derbyshire
One of a series of similar ceremonies carried out around this season in neighbouring Derbyshire villages. The village wells are decorated (often very elaborately) with leaves, branches and flowers pressed in clay to depict themes from the Bible. The vicar leads a procession from well to well holding thanksgiving services for supplying pure water throughout the previous year.

*May 29 Oak Apple Day or Garland King Day
Castleton, Derbyshire
Almost certainly an old May Day rite, which has now become attached to Oak Apple Day – on which the Restoration of Charles II in 1660 is celebrated. (The Oak Apple referring to the famous incident when Charles hid in an oak tree to elude the searching Roundhead troops after the Battle of Worcester.) The celebrations here include many traditional May Day features and several unique to the village. There is a procession led by a 'King' and 'Lady' with a beehive made of wild flowers carried on horseback, and later children dance around a maypole.

4th week in May **The Siege of Belton**
Grantham, Lincolnshire
Belton House is set in 600 acres of fine parkland, and here they hold an annual full-dress re-enactment of the Civil War Siege of Belton. Throughout the summer there are also exciting re-enactments of such historic events as the Battle of Gettysburg from the American Civil War, complete with cannons, much gunsmoke and valiant deeds.

*Jun 29 Hay & Rush Strewing Ceremonies
Barrowden and Braunstone, Leicestershire
These customs stem from the ancient practice of changing the rushes or hay (used instead of carpets) in the church each year. At Barrowden, rushes from the nearby fields are strewn on the floor of the church. At Braunstone, the ceremony takes place on the nearest Sunday to Jun 29 – only here the

modern world has caught up with an ancient ritual. A previous Lord Mayor left a legacy to the church providing hay from his nearby fields. But the fields are now covered with a gasworks, and the East Midlands Gas Board pays cash instead of the original hay! However, the ancient service remains celebrated – an all too rare example of how an old custom has survived modern industrialisation.

*1st week in Oct Goose Fair
Recreation Ground, Nottingham
Originally a Michaelmas Fair, where farmers came to sell their geese, the traditional dish at this time of year. This fair has been going since 1542 and is one of the best-known in the country, having accumulated all kinds of local folklore. Nowadays it is purely a funfair – but none the worse for that – attracting huge crowds.

Dec 21 Candle Auction
Old Bolingbroke, Lincolnshire
A traditional St Thomas Day charity, one of the few remaining of a much more widespread custom. A piece of land called 'Poor Folks Close' is let once every five years by the ancient method of candle auctioning (which is described by the diarist Samuel Pepys). The vicar sticks a pin into a lighted candle and the bidding for the grazing rights of the land begins. The last bidder before the pin falls out wins the auction.

Dec Laxton Jury Day & Court Leet
Laxton, Nottinghamshire
The only village in England which still uses the old feudal system farming method – with strips in different fields owned by each of the villagers. These fields are administered by a field jury who report to the Court Leet, where judgment is made on farming policy. The manor is now run by the Ministry of Agriculture.

3rd Sun in Dec Tin Can Band
Broughton, Northamptonshire
An ancient custom with its origins in a primitive and far from pleasant rite, dating from the days of superstition and witchcraft. Centuries ago, a gypsy woman gave birth to an illegitimate child on the outskirts of the village. Since then, it has been customary for the village lads to gather outside the church, and on the stroke of midnight to proceed around the village banging dustbin lids, kettles and tin plates – allegedly to frighten off the gypsies, who were thought to cast evil spells.

West Midlands and Welsh Borders

*Shrove Tuesday Shrovetide Football
Atherstone, West Midlands
An ancient example of football, said to have started in this particular case in the 13th c. during the reign of King John. Originally men-at-arms from Leicestershire and Warwickshire played for a prize of a bag of gold. Nowadays the two local teams play with a water-filled football which is decorated with the local colours.

Palm Sunday Distribution of Pax Cakes
Sellack and Kings Caple, Herefordshire
A quaint local custom initiated in the 16th c. by a certain Lady Scudamore. She distributed cakes and ale amongst the villagers because she believed that all those who shared a meal on Palm Sunday would not quarrel during the coming year. Despite the frailties of human nature, these celebrations optimistically continue.

Apr 23 Shakespeare's Birthday Celebrations
Stratford-upon-Avon, West Midlands
Despite widespread commercialisation, with souvenirs and seasons of plays at the Memorial Theatre attended by international conferences, Stratford still manages to celebrate its most famous son in inimitable style.

On Apr 23 (which oddly is the day of Shakespeare's death as well as his birth) a procession with flags of many nations makes its way down Bridge Street to the 'Swan of Avon's' grave, where wreaths are laid.

4th week in May Hereford Cider Festival

The Cider Grounds, Herefordshire
Celebration of Herefordshire's ancient industry, with a Market Fayre attended by ladies in traditional costume. All kinds of apple goods sold at the stalls – toffee apples, local apple pies, and a wide range of ciders.

May 28 Court of Arraye & Bower Procession

Lichfield, Staffordshire
According to an ancient charter, each year the city of Lichfield had to provide a certain amount of armour for the Crown, for use in the King's army. Through the ages, this ancient provision became associated with a local medieval pleasure fair known as 'the Bower'. Nowadays there is a procession with local youths dressed in suits of armour, who then line up for inspection by the town officials.

May 29 Arbour Tree Day

Aston on Clun, Salop
A peculiar local custom in which a black poplar tree is adorned with flags. This is said to mark the wedding of Mary Charter and John Marston, which took place at Aston on Clun in 1786. However, many historians believe the custom in fact originates from the earlier worship of St Bridget, who 'took over' from an ancient pagan goddess whose shrine was near where the tree now stands.

**4th week in Jun* Droitwich Gala

Droitwich, Worcestershire
The remnants of an ancient Midsummer Fair. The week-long gala, which centres around the Lido Park, features many medieval games, and all kinds of historical re-enactments – including, for some reason, cowboys and Indians on horseback.

Jul Madley Festival

Madley, Herefordshire
A week-long music festival, which also features art exhibitions and craft shows. The festival centres around the 13th-c. Madley parish church, which lies amidst the magnificent countryside of the Wye valley. A typical, unpretentious country festival attended largely by people from the surrounding area.

Mon in early Sep Abbots Bromley Horn Dance

Abbots Bromley, Staffordshire
The origins of this dance are lost in time – though according to one legend it marks the granting of hunting privileges in Needwood Forest to the village during Norman times. However, it seems more likely that the origins of this strange dance go back to a pre-Christian pagan cult. The dancers wear reindeer horns and are accompanied by such traditional characters as the Fool, a Hobby Horse and Robin Hood (who often took the place of the Green Man). The procession makes its way to farmhouses and cottages throughout the parish, and ends up in the local inn, where they drink the traditional toast: 'The Horn Dance of Abbey Bromley, long may it continue!'

Sep 4 The Sheriff's Ride

Lichfield, Staffordshire
According to a charter granted to Lichfield by Mary Tudor in 1553, the Sheriff must make a tour of the boundaries of the city on the Feast of the Nativity of the Blessed Virgin Mary to see that none of the boundary stones has been tampered with. In former times, the procession would set out on horseback to cover the 24 miles of the city's boundaries, with special watchers posted to see that no one took any short cuts home. Nowadays an abbreviated formal parade goes through the streets to the Guildhall.

Sat nearest Sep 18 **Samuel Johnson's Birthday Celebrations**
Lichfield, Staffordshire
Celebrations to commemorate the birthday in 1709 of the man who compiled the first English dictionary, the famous wit and writer Dr Johnson. In the morning there is a procession, followed by the laying of a wreath at Dr Johnson's statue by the Mayor and Sheriff. Later in the evening local dignitaries attend a commemoration supper where they dine on Dr Johnson's favourite menu: steak and kidney pudding, apple tart with cream, ale and hot punch.

On the Monday following this birthday celebration there is a ceremony in Uttoxeter, where a wreath is laid by a plaque fixed to the wall of an old stone kiosk in the Market Place. This is where Johnson is said to have been made to stand as a penance for disobedience in his youth (an event he may well have wished to forget during his own lifetime, let alone have remembered over 250 years later!).

*Oct 12 (& 26) **Mop Fair (& Runaway Mop Fair)**
Stratford-upon-Avon, West Midlands
Remnants of an ancient Mop Fair, where domestic servants stood with mops (the emblem of their trade) plying for hire, along with other labourers such as shepherds and carters. Nowadays this is more of a funfair, where a whole ox is roasted amidst customary jollities.

A fortnight later there is the Runaway Mop Fair. In the old days this was held ten days after the original fair, to give anyone that was dissatisfied with the master who had hired them a chance to find new employment for the year.

Horn Dancers of Abbots Bromley

Nov 11 **Wroth Silver Plaid**
Knightlow Hill, West Midlands
An ancient custom whereby the representatives of the parishes that make up the Hundred meet with an agent of the Duke of Buccleuch. After the agent has read out the ancient charter, each of the parish representatives must pay an appointed sum (around 10p), placing it on a stone called the 'Knightlow Cross'. This money is called the 'Wroth Silver', and anyone not paying is fined £1 for every penny not paid, or must give the Duke a white bull with a red nose and red ears.

North-West

Good Friday **Burning Judas**
Liverpool, Merseyside
A ceremony which contains an amalgam of ancient customs. At first light on Good Friday the children of the South End of Liverpool appear with a 'Judas' made out of old clothes stuffed with straw. This is carried through the streets on a pole, while the children beg for pennies at the houses. Later, the effigy is ceremonially burnt.

Easter Monday **Nutters' Dance**
Bacup, Lancashire
The eight Coconutters with blackened hands and faces, wearing their peculiar outfits, perform a succession of highly skilled dances through the streets, accompanied by the town band. Part of their dancing involves clapping together wooden discs attached to their hands and knees, which produce an ingenious rhythmic effect. These small discs are known as 'coconuts', but are in fact the tops of cotton bobbins. The dancers are still sometimes called the 'Britannia Coco-Nut Dancers', as the nine-man troupe originally consisted of men from the Britannia Mill.

Easter Monday **Riding the Black Lad**
Ashton-under-Lyme, Lancashire
The origins of this ceremony are said to date from a specific incident in the 14th c., when Edward III made Thomas Ashton a knight. This proved

highly unpopular with the locals, and they have persisted in venting their displeasure ever since by making a 'guy' out of a stuffed old suit and parading it around the town on a horse. After this, the effigy is tied to a post and set on fire. However, the custom almost certainly has even earlier origins in a pre-Christian fertility rite.

★Easter **Easter Customs**
West Derby and Bury, Lancashire
In the last century, the poor men of West Derby would congregate on Easter Sunday wearing ragged clothes, to make a round of the houses to collect charity in the form of oatmeal, cakes, money and eggs (for egg rolling). Nowadays it is customary for the men to wear their clothes inside out, with coloured patches, and go from door to door collecting alms. They then retire to the pub for a celebration.

In Bury on Easter Monday, a group from the local folk club put on an original and authentic version of a Mummers' Play – the Easter Pace Egg Play – in the shopping precincts and pubs around the town.

★Sat after May 1 **Royal May Day**
Knutsford, Cheshire
Part of the celebrations involved here commemorate an event which took place in 1017, when King Canute won a great local victory. However, the present festivities date only from 1864. Amongst the celebrations is the crowning of a May Queen and a typical May Day procession. A unique element here is the sand paintings which are made on the streets, consisting of elaborate arabesques and mottos in coloured sand.

Fri nearest Jun 30 **Warrington Walk Day**
Warrington, Lancashire
This custom was started in 1832 by the Rector of Warrington, the Rev. H. Powys. His idea was to organise the children of the town in a 'procession of witness' to divert local attention from

the alternative joys of the Latchford and Newton races, which were held on the same day. Nowadays the procession still includes groups from the local Sunday schools, but it has become more of a carnival – with the children dressing up and carrying garlands of flowers and balloons.

Jul 5 **Tynwald Parliament**
St John's, Isle of Man

The Tynwald is the parliament of the Isle of Man, and according to the island's constitution no law has validity on the island until it has been passed at the open-air parliament meeting on Tynwald Hill. The Tynwald is over 1000 years old and meets each year on the old Midsummer's Day. The Tynwald Hill itself is a small man-made knoll, 12ft high and 85ft in diameter, which contains soil from the 17 parishes of the island. At the Tynwald the acts which have been passed at Westminster in the previous year are read out in Manx (the ancient Gaelic language of the Isle) and these then become law in the Isle of Man.

★Jul 5 **Bawming the Thorn**
Appleton, Cheshire

The present thorn tree in the centre of the village is less than 20 years old, though its predecessor (around which the original custom grew) was many centuries old. It was said to have been taken as a cutting from the Holy Thorn in Glastonbury by one Adam de Dutton in 1125, who planted it in Appleton. The thorn then became the focus for several old midsummer rites, and the custom grew up of adorning the trees with ribbons and garlands. Afterwards, the village children would join hands and dance around the base of the tree. This custom is still carried out on the old Midsummer's Day (of the pre-1752 calendar).

★From Aug 24 **Wakes Week**
Westhoughton, Lancashire

Until a few decades ago Wakes Weeks were traditionally the time when the mills would close down all over Lancashire and the workers would go on holiday. This Wakes Week begins on St Bartholomew's Day and includes a wide variety of sporting events and entertainments, many of which stem from the old custom of holding Bartholomew Fairs. In previous centuries it was traditional here to bake a large pie in the shape of a cow's head, and for this reason the inhabitants of Westhoughton are still sometimes affectionately known as 'Cow-heads'.

2nd week Sep-early Oct **Blackpool Illuminations**
Blackpool, Lancashire

These illuminations started in 1912 as part of the town's Music Festival, and are now as much a part of Northern folklore as Donald McGill postcards and black pudding. The illuminations consist of six miles of lights along the promenade, and these are ceremonially switched on each year, usually by a famous personality. Despite now being put on after the high season, the lights continue to attract huge crowds.

Oct **Cheshire Ploughing Match**
Malpas, Cheshire

Originally, ploughing matches of this sort were held all over the country. Now this is one of the few remaining in England. Here, as well as more mechanical ploughing, you can see ploughmen of the old breed using traditional shares and pairs of heavy horses. Not only a fast-disappearing traditional sight, but also a fascinating exhibition of rural skills.

★Early Nov **Souling & Soul Caking Day**
Antrobus and Comberbach, Cheshire

In previous centuries, it was the custom to collect cakes on All Saints' Day for the souls of the dead. Nowadays, the children still go round the houses begging for Soul Cakes (or 'Dole Bread' as it is sometimes called). Also at this time of year the villagers put on a special Soul Caking Play. This was once a regular custom all over North Cheshire, and this last remaining example still contains the traditional Hoodening (or wild) Horse.

Yorkshire

Nightly **Horn Blowing Ceremony**
Ripon, North Yorkshire
This custom derives from the old curfew, which was once strictly observed in Ripon each night. At 9 the Hornblower (an official appointed by the Mayor) goes to the Mayor's house and blows the horn, and then proceeds to the Market Place where he blows the horn four times. The custom is said to have originated in Saxon times, when a Wakeman (who was responsible for keeping order in the town) was required to blow the horn each evening at sunset to mark the start of the curfew.

★Sat in early Jan **Goathland Plough Stots**
Goathland, North Yorkshire
This custom is a revival of ancient Plough Monday practices. There is a procession through the village, led by a 'Lord' and 'Lady', together with a group of musicians, sword dancers and men in fantastic disguises (known as 'toms'). Also accompanying the procession are the 'plough stots' – the local lads, leading a bullock, who stop at the houses collecting money for charity.

★Shrove Tuesday **Shrovetide Skipping**
Scarborough, North Yorkshire
A unique custom, which stems from centuries ago when Shrove Tuesday used to be known in these parts as 'Ball Day'. At that time the locals would gather on the beach and play ball games of all kinds to let off steam before the austerities of the Lenten fast. Nowadays large crowds, consisting of young and old alike, congregate in the afternoon on the Southsands Promenade with skipping ropes and hold all kinds of skipping games until dusk. Believe it or not, it's still a common sight to see rows of half a dozen jolly fishermen skipping as their wives twirl the long ropes!

★Shrove Tuesday **Ringing the Pancake Bell**
Scarborough, North Yorkshire
Over a hundred years ago a big bell called the Curfew Bell used to hang at the entrance of St Thomas the Matre Hospital. This was rung at midday on Shrove Tuesday to remind everyone to start frying their traditional pancakes. In 1861 the hospital was pulled down, but the bell was removed to the town museum, where it still hangs, and is religiously rung by the staff each Shrove Tuesday.

3rd Thur in Mar **Kiplingcotes Derby**
Market Weighton, Humberside
This is a horse race in the style of the old point-to-points, except that there are no jumps. As such it is claimed to be the oldest flat race in the country, having started in 1519. The traditional course is over 4 miles and runs through several parishes between South Dalton and Kiplingcotes Farm. All the contesting riders pay a £4 stake and must weigh over 10 stone. (They are weighed before the race on a coal merchant's scales – and made to empty their pockets of any heavy objects beforehand.) The winner of the race receives the interest of some stock which was purchased as a prize by Lord Burlington in 1618, and the second rider receives all the stake money. As Lord Burlington's interest now only comes to around £5, there is always a great battle for second place!

★Easter Monday & Whit Tuesday **Maypole Raising**
Barwick in Elmet, West Yorkshire
This village claims to have the tallest maypole in Britain, and every three years it is taken down with much ceremony on Easter Monday to be repainted. On Whit Tuesday it is raised again, with four new garlands. After this, there is a traditional May Day celebration, with a procession which ends up at Hall Tower Field where the May Queen is crowned and the maypole dancing begins. (The celebrations take place each year.)

Easter Monday **World Coal Carrying Championships**
Dewsbury, West Yorkshire
A traditional race which remains popular with tough local miners. The contestants run over a prescribed course, each carrying a large sack of coal on their shoulders. Mere mortals find these sacks difficult enough to pick up, let alone run with – and the race occasionally produces spectacular 'spills'!

★*Ascensiontide* **Planting the Penny Hedge (or Horngarth)**
Whitby, North Yorkshire
A curious ancient custom which takes place on the Eve of Ascension. It is said to date from a penance, which was imposed on three local noblemen in 1159 after they had behaved in an unruly fashion and beaten up the local hermit. The noblemen were ordered to construct along the low tide mark a horngarth (a hedge of stakes) sturdy enough to last the rise and fall of three tides. Over 800 years later, the locals still keep up the penance.

Last week in Jul–1st 2 weeks in Aug **Harrogate Festival**
Harrogate, North Yorkshire
This is the Festival's 18th year and it gets steadily larger and grander. There are many concerts and recitals, and there's also a literary festival, following hard on the heels of the one-week literary festival in Ilkley, West Yorkshire.
See *Festivals*, p. 94

1st Tues in Aug **Ancient Gooseberry Contest**
Whitby, North Yorkshire
This is held at Egton Bridge, and is one of the most ancient horticultural events in the land. Amidst a carnival atmosphere the contesting gardeners have their gooseberries judged and weighed. Many of them weigh over 2oz and often attain the size of hens' eggs (using many jealously guarded local gardeners' secrets, some of which are handed down from father to son).

★*Sat after Aug 24* **Burning Bartle**
West Witton, North Yorkshire
An ancient St Bartholomew's Day celebration which has somehow become associated with a notorious thief who was caught in the neighbourhood several centuries ago. The villagers carry in procession a large straw effigy which is known as 'Bartle'. To the accompaniment of a traditional rhyme about the catching of the thief, the villagers make their way down the main street. Afterwards the effigy is ritually stabbed and then set on fire. The name 'Bartle' stems from St Bartholomew – but the effigy is said to represent the thief.

Dec 24 **Tolling the Devil's Bell**
Dewsbury, West Yorkshire
In the 13th c. a local gentleman called Thomas de Soothill killed one of his servants. As a penance, Thomas gave a bell (now known as 'Black Tom of Soothill') to the local church, and ordered the bell to be rung on Christmas Eve each year to remind him of his sin. Now, by tradition, the bell is tolled once for each year since Christ was born, with the last toll being made to coincide with the midnight chimes marking the start of Christmas Day. The number of tolls is meticulously ticked off on a large pad. This custom is said to keep the Devil out of the parish during the next 12 months.

North

★*Shrove Tuesday* **Shrovetide Football**
Sedgefield, Durham
Traditional rough-house football played with a specially-made ball slightly larger than a hockey ball. The pitch consists of a 500-yard stretch of land between a stream and a pond. The local verger starts the game at 1pm by throwing the ball into the air, and the game is over when either side scores a goal, by getting the ball into the stream or the pond.

Good Friday **Pram Races**

Sunderland and various towns and villages around Tyneside

These races were once a traditional Eastertide sport all over the North of England, and they still remain popular in Tyneside and parts of North Yorkshire. The contestants are expected to dress up, and the 'baby' in the pram takes his life into his hands as his partner hurtles down the street with the other contestants in true Ben Hur style.

Wed nearest May 18 **Dunting the Freeholder**

Newbiggin-by-the-Sea, Northumberland

An ancient custom which is claimed locally to have its origins in medieval times. The villagers hold freehold 'stints' (pieces of land) on nearby Newbiggin Moor. Each time a new freeholder takes over his stint he is initiated at the 'Dunting Stone' on the moor. This was once a Druid stone, but is now a concrete pillar. Some local historians believe that this ancient practice is almost certainly an echo of some pre-Christian sacrificial rite, whose precise significance has long been forgotten.

★4th week in Jun **Alnwick Fair**

Alnwick, Northumberland

This fair is held in the Market Square, and has revived many of the ancient practices of the old 18th-c. Spring Hiring Fairs, where servants and farm labourers came in from the surrounding countryside to seek employment for the coming year. Nowadays the fair has a particularly jolly carnival atmosphere, with people in traditional costume taking part in such ancient rituals as 'ducking the maid' (in a pool of water).

★Sat in Jul **Ambleside Rushbearing Ceremony**

Ambleside, Cumbria

This ceremony takes place in St Mary's Church on the nearest Saturday to St Anne's Day. In bygone times, the rushes strewn on the beaten earth of the church floor (in place of carpets) were changed annually at this time of year. Nowadays, the rushes are carried in procession through the town to the Market Place, where the congregation sing the traditional Rushbearing Hymn. Afterwards, everyone who has carried the rushes is rewarded with a customary slice of gingerbread.

3rd week in Jul **Durham Miners' Gala**

Durham

Gala weeks are still held all over the north of England. Once these marked the annual miners' holidays. Nowadays there are funfairs, processions with brass bands and carnivals, and the most famous of them all at Durham has the Durham races as well. This gala is traditionally attended by luminaries from the Labour Party and the trade union movement, who stand on the balcony waving to the crowds as the best brass bands in the world blare down the street.

Sat nearest Sep 18 **Crabapple Fair**

Egremont, Cumbria

This fair, which may well have once been a traditional Michaelmas Fair, has been held since 1267 and still retains many traditional features. Amongst the sports available there are climbing the greasy pole and scrambling for pennies. Pipe smoking and singing contests are also held. But this fair is perhaps best known for its World Champion Gurning Competition, in which the competitors all attempt to contort their faces into ugly grimaces and fantastic expressions. The winner with the ugliest face (or 'gurn') is awarded a cup and crowned with a special horse harness.

★Dec 31 **Tar-barrel Parade**

Allendale, Northumberland

This parade incorporates a number of traditional New Year customs which were once popular throughout the country. The procession is mentioned in the records in 1884, but has probably been going for much longer.

The 'guisers' in fancy dress carry the barrels from the church to the Market Place accompanied by the town band. Here the barrels are lit, and the assembled company sings 'Auld Lang Syne'. Afterwards people set off to go 'First Footing' around the houses of their friends.

Wales

1st week in Jan Mary Lwyd
Various towns and villages, especially in Glamorgan

Traditional Yuletide jollities with many local variations, but always involving a variety of hobby horse. The horse itself it made from a horse's skull decorated with ribbons. The origins and practices of this custom are similar to those of the Padstow Hobby Horse.

*Mar 1 St David's Day
St Davids, Dyfed, and all over Wales

St David is the patron saint of Wales, and St David's Day is very much the Welsh National Day, with the emphasis on traditional Welsh emblems such as leeks and daffodils. There are celebrations of all kinds all over Wales. Amongst other customs it is traditional for all the soldiers of the Welsh Regiments to be presented with a leek at a formal ceremony.

At St David's Cathedral they hold a special commemorative service for St David, who is said to have settled in this part of Wales in the 6th c. and established a major Christian centre.

Mar 1 Leek Sergeant Ceremony
Mountwood, Llanfoist, Powys

A rather primitive military interpretation of an ancient custom. On St David's Day the five newest recruits at the barracks here are presented with five raw leeks on a silver salver by their sergeant – whereupon they are made to eat them, there and then. This practice stems from the ancient belief that anyone who hasn't eaten a leek is not a proper Welshman.

*May or Jun May Day Celebrations
Rhyl, Clwyd

A typical local May Day celebration which no longer takes place on May Day itself. The week-long festivities include all kinds of traditional events, with fancy dress pageants and Morris dancing. The celebrations culminate in a grand parade led by the May Queen and her young attendants in fancy dress.

*Whitsuntide Common Walk
Laugharne, Dyfed

A traditional 'Beating of the Bounds' ceremony, with the Mayor and his officials leading a procession of townsfolk round the corporation boundaries of this beautiful town overlooking the estuary of the River Taf. (It was here that the great Welsh poet Dylan Thomas wrote much of his poetry, and he is buried in the local graveyard.)

*Rogationtide Blessing the Fields
Castle Caereinion, Powys

A unique custom involving the Llanfair Light Railway which runs between Welshpool and Llanfair Caereinion. A service is celebrated on board the train by the vicar of St Mary's Church, and prayers are said at every station the train stops at along the line. A curious modern version of an ancient springtime rite.

Jun Cardigan Eisteddfod
Cardigan, Dyfed

A revival of an ancient Welsh cultural custom with the aim of fostering Welsh arts, music and language. One of the chief elements here is the chairing of the bard, when the winning poet is presented with flowers by young girls in ceremonial dress.

Eisteddfods are competitive gatherings for singers, musicians and poets, and the language used is exclusively Welsh. The first recorded Eisteddfod was held in the 6th c. at Conway, though there had certainly been many before this. Historians believe these gatherings originate from the ancient Druid conclaves. The custom of holding Eisteddfods was revived at the end of the 18th c., and they quickly became a popular national focus. The biggest event of all is the National Eisteddfod, which is held at the beginning of August at a different venue each year.

1st week in Jul International Musical Eisteddfod
Llangollen, Clwyd

This cultural gathering was established over 30 years ago and has since developed into the greatest folk-dancing festival in the world. Nowadays it often attracts as many as 10,000 competitors. Visitors from remote regions of countries all over the globe compete, performing authentic dances, playing traditional instruments and wearing national costumes. There are also competitions for purely vocal or instrumental groups. A unique opportunity to see examples of a fast-fading heritage.

Jul Royal Welsh Show
Llanelwedd, Powys

One of Britain's best-known agricultural shows, which takes place amidst some of the finest scenery in Wales. All the usual agricultural elements are featured, including a parade of champions, show-jumping and livestock competitions of many kinds.

1st & 2nd week in Aug, alternate years Cardiff Searchlight Tattoo

The floodlit court of Cardiff Castle is a dramatic setting for this military pageant with its massed bands and displays of precision marching.

4th week in Aug Monmouthshire Show
Monmouth, Gwent

A typical country town show, set amidst the picturesque rolling countryside of the Wye valley. All kinds of agricultural and funfair events amidst a boisterous carnival atmosphere, which attracts farmers and children alike from all over the country.

Aug 29 Beca Mountain Race
Mynachlogddu region of Presli, Dyfed

A strange commemorative celebration mixing endurance, tradition and slapstick. This race commemorates the Rebecca Riots which took place locally in the last century. The competitors have to run up the mountain and down again. The winner is the first one down who can change into women's clothing and then chop down a facsimile toll-gate with an axe.

*Nov The Dunmow Flitch
Crickhowell, Powys

A copy of the trial held at Dunmow in Essex. However, here the proceedings are slightly more farcical. The four couples who compete for the flitch (side of bacon) must convince a joke judge and roistering jury that they have been happily married throughout the previous year and a day.

Near Christmas Torchlight Procession
Brymaur, Powys

Owing to the strong Nonconformist tradition, such events as torchlight processions are a rarity in Wales. One of the few remaining is at Brymaur, where the villagers parade through the streets with candles to sing Christmas carols.

Dec 26 Boxing Day Swim
Tenby, Dyfed

This particular custom is a mere ten years old, but increases in popularity each year – with both participants and spectators. Hundreds of intrepid bathers, many in weird and wonderful garb, gather at the North Beach. On the appointed signal, there is a lemming-like charge into the icy water – accompanied by customary high-pitched squealing. Determined masochists often last in the water for several minutes before being helped blue-skinned and staggering back up the beach, muttering the traditional responses about having really enjoyed themselves.

Scottish Lowlands

Jan 25 **Burns' Night Celebrations**
Ayr and all over Scotland

Robert 'Rabbie' Burns is Scotland's national poet, and throughout Scotland or wherever a group of Scots find themselves together in exile, it is customary to celebrate with a special dinner on Burns' Night. The central feature of these celebrations is the 'piping in of the haggis'. This dish is made of the heart and liver of sheep mixed with oatmeal and seasoning stuffed into a sheep's stomach and is traditionally saved with 'neeps' (turnips) and whisky. It is carried in by the chef, to the accompaniment of the stirring music of bagpipes played by kilted pipers. As a prelude to the ceremonial cutting of the haggis it is customary to recite Burns celebrated 'Ode to a Haggis'. This celebration is kept alive by the many Burns Clubs, the first of which was founded in 1802 in Greenock (eight years after the poet's death). Now there are over 700 of these clubs all over the world, and in many ways Burns' Night has become the Scottish national celebration.

Mar 1 **Whuppity Scoorie**
Lanark, Strathclyde

A unique custom centred on the local parish church. As the church bell tolls, the local children run three times round the church and then engage in a mock battle with paper balls attached to pieces of string. The proceedings are further enlivened when the local councillors toss handfuls of coins into the fray, and a mass scramble ensues. This custom almost certainly originates from a pagan rite to ward off evil spirits, which formed part of a springtime festival. However, there is also a picturesque local explanation. In bygone times the convicts from the local gaol were taken out on Mar 1 to have their annual wash in the nearby

Burns' Night Dinner

Clyde. Prior to the bath (or perhaps to encourage full enthusiasm in this all too necessary hygienic ritual) the prisoners were first whipped. This would account for naming the day 'Whuppity Scoorie' (local dialect for 'whipping and scouring').

Apr **Kate Kennedy Celebrations**
St Andrews, Fife
The original Kate Kennedy was the niece of the founder of St Andrews University, and was renowned locally for her beauty. Each year, as part of these celebrations at the University, a first-year student plays the part of Kate in an elaborate historical pageant which attracts large crowds of students and locals.

May or Jun **Raft Races**
Kelso, Borders
Raft races were once a popular annual custom on many rivers throughout Britain. To this day they remain widespread in Scotland. In this particular race improvised rafts of all shapes and sizes race down the River Tweed from Kelso to Carnham.

1st Sat in Jun **John Newland's Day**
Bathgate, Lothian
This annual celebration commemorates the town's great benefactor. John Newland emigrated to seek his fortune, and when he returned home a rich man he gave money for the building of schools, a library and many other civic services.

1st week in Jun **Scottish National Opera Proms**
Edinburgh, Lothian
The Scottish equivalent of London's Promenade Season. These concerts are held in the Usher Hall, and end in the traditional revelries of the 'Last Night of the Proms'. The concerts range through all kinds of classical music, with a special emphasis on Scots, or Scots-orientated music.

*Jun 23 **Beltane Feast**
Peebles, Borders
Beltane was an ancient Celtic festival associated with fire (the Gaelic *beallteinn* means 'goodly fire'). This festival features a revival of an ancient firelighting ceremony, more usually associated with May 1 in other regions. Also, on the steps of the old parish church a child is crowned the Beltane Queen, and her train is carried by a troupe of children in ceremonial attire. This is followed by the Riding of the Marches.

Jul **Braw Lads Gathering**
Galashiels, Borders
A two-day festival which celebrates events from the town's history with much horseback pageantry. The big feature here is a re-enactment of the defeat of the English in 1337 by the local 'Braw Lads' (brave lads).

Early Jul **Herring Queen Week**
Eyemouth, Borders
A typical local carnival week, where the high point is the landing of the Herring Queen, which takes place at the Gungsgreen area of the harbour. A procession of local fishing boats, decked in flags and bunting, sails in with the Herring Queen and her attendant maidens in flowing robes – who then disembark for the official crowning ceremony.

Thur in late Aug **Race for the Red Hose**
Carnwarth, Strathclyde
Claimed by the locals to be the oldest running race in Europe. The race itself dates from a charter issued by James IV of Scotland on Mar 13 1508. The course is a mile long, and the winner receives a locally knitted pair of red stockings and a small sum of money. In previous centuries it was decreed that the winner's name should be publicly proclaimed at the Mercat Cross in Edinburgh, but this part of the custom has now lapsed and the race is simply a feature of the local Highland Games and Cattle Show.

Early Aug **Burry Man's Day**
South Queensferry, Lothian
A unique local custom which involves a man covered from head to toe in

Scottish piper

burdock burrs, supported by two poles which are decorated with flowers. This 'Burry Man' who parades through the streets is said to have originated from a shipwrecked sailor who had no clothes and covered himself in burrs.

★2nd week in Aug **Lammas Fair**
St Andrews, Fife
An annual Lammas-tide fair, which in centuries gone by attracted farmers from all over the country. Now it is mainly a funfair, but remains nonetheless a highly popular traditional gathering.

Late Aug **World Flounder-Trampling Championship**
Palnackie, Dumfries & Galloway
A curious and increasingly popular annual custom which has many of the features of an ancient ritual – though it only began in the 1970s as a charity event. The participants wade through the shallow waters of the Urr estuary on the Solway Firth when the tide is out with the aim of trampling on flounder fish. As soon as one of the participants feels a flounder wriggling underfoot he spears it with an improvised trident made out of a fork tied to a piece of bamboo. After much wading, trampling and stabbing the World Champion is eventually proclaimed!

Last week in Aug-1st week in Sep **Edinburgh Festival**
Edinburgh, Lothian
One of the world's major cultural festivals, attracting international artists. The events include concerts, exhibitions, films, literary readings and a wide range of theatrical performances. There is also the celebrated Fringe Festival, which features all kinds of alternative, *avant-garde* and zany activities of a mainly theatrical nature. (One year this included a 'theatre company' which performed for an audience of one inside a travelling taxi!) Other events include the famous Military Tattoo at Edinburgh Castle, which features Highland pipers parading under floodlights beneath the castle battlements. The artistic events at this festival are of an excellence and variety such as is found at no other cultural festival in the world – particularly in the fields of opera and theatre. Events of all kinds go on around the clock, and it is often necessary to book well in advance for the 'high spots'.
See *Festivals*, p. 94

1st or 2nd week in Sep **Viking Festival**
Largs, Strathclyde
A week-long carnival at one of Glasgow's main seaside holiday resorts. Events include fireworks, processions and all kinds of entertainments and cultural events. The high point is the great re-enactment of the Battle of Largs, with much heroism and gruesomely authentic fighting between opponents in period costume. The battle harks back to the dark days of the 13th c. when the whole of Scotland was plagued by Viking invaders from Scandinavia and Iceland. However, when King Haakon of Norway landed at Largs he met fierce resistance and was driven back into the sea.

Up-Helly-A

Scottish Highlands and Islands

★Jan 1 **Kirkwall Ba' Games**
Kirkwall, Orkney

A typical rough-house football game, with precious few rules, such as used to be played all over the country – more usually on Shrove Tuesday. This takes place on the streets of Kirkwall and attracts hundreds of boisterous participants of all ages. Often you can only tell where the ball is by spotting where the scrum is most violent!

Jan 11 **Burning the Clavie**
Burghead, Grampian

This custom dates from a pre-Christian fire rite, believed to have been practised locally by Druids. A tar-barrel is set alight by the 'Clavie King' and is then carried in procession through the town. After this, the burning barrel is placed in position on Loorie Hill – where in former times the flames were believed to ward off evil spirits.

Last Tue in Jan **Up-Helly-A**
Lerwick, Shetland
With this famous custom the hardy
Shetlanders celebrate their Nordic
ancestry. (Lerwick is in fact as close to
Bergen in Norway as it is to
Aberdeen.) The celebrations
originated as a Viking Fire Festival
marking the end of Yuletide (Up-
Helly-A is thought to be a local
corruption of a Scandinavian name).
Hundreds of Shetlanders dressed as
Vikings, wearing helmets and carrying
shields and axes, assemble at Market
Cross at 9pm. There is then a
torchlight procession through the
streets with a 30ft Viking long-boat.
Later the long-boat is set on fire
amidst typical midwinter revelries.
One of Britain's most spectacular – and
convivial – traditional celebrations.

4th week in Mar **Snow Fun Week**
Glenshee, Tayside
A carnival mixture of traditional and
modern events, fun and games in the
main ski-ing region north of Perth.
Entertainments include tobogganing,
ski-ing and the building of snowmen,
and in the evenings there are folk
nights, dances and ceilidhs (traditional
musical evenings). A week-long winter
fun festival with a difference, which is
highly popular with all ages.

Mid Jun **World Caber-Tossing
Championships**
Aberdeen, Grampian
For the uninitiated this looks like a
group of ox-like men in kilts heaving
telegraph poles – though for those who
know, it is a game of real skill, as well
as great strength. The World Caber-
Tossing Championships are the high
spot of the Aberdeen Highland Games
at Hazelhead Park and often attract
participants of Scots descent from as
far afield as Canada.

Mid Jun **Festival of Ceilidhs**
Keith, Grampian
This festival is organised by the
Traditional Music and Song
Association of Scotland, and provides a
perfect opportunity to sample the
living musical heritage of the Scots. All
kinds of events are staged, but the
emphasis is on fiddle-playing and
traditional singing. A unique occasion
for the devotees of local music – and a
great atmosphere, in which the thirsty
participants mingle with the audience.

Late Jun-early Jul **Seafood Festival**
Tarbert, Strathclyde
Officially entitled 'The Tarbert Loch
Fyne Seafood Festival', this event
includes all kinds of entertainments
and sports, including concerts, a
fishing boat parade, tug-o-war and the
crowning of a Seafood Queen. There is
also a boisterous Raft Race. At the
same time the traditional Tarbert Fair
takes place along the picturesque
harbour front. This is now purely a
funfair, but was originated by an Act
passed by the Scottish Parliament in
1705.

Mid Aug **Strathpeffer Highland
Games**
Strathpeffer, Highland
The annual gathering at Castle Leod.
The games include all the traditional
events, such as putting the shot,
tossing the caber, sword dancing and
bagpipe playing – all amidst the finest
highland scenery.

Late Aug or early Sep **Arbroath Abbey
Pageant**
Arbroath, Tayside
This traditional historical pageant
commemorates the Scottish
Declaration of Independence in the
14th c. by King Robert the Bruce (who
routed the English at Bannockburn).
Amidst much patriotic pomp and
ceremony the original document was
signed on Apr 6, 1320, in the Abbey of
Arbroath, and this ceremony is re-
enacted in authentic detail amidst the
ruins of the old Abbey. In the town
there are also a series of traditional
entertainments called *Fit o' the
Toon* – light-hearted events put on by
the locals of the famous fishing
community.

Early Sep **Ben Nevis Hill Race**
Fort William, Highland
A tough traditional cross-country
event up and down the tallest
mountain in Britain, whose 4406ft
peak overlooks Fort William. Amidst
rugged highland scenery the hundreds
of massed competitors charge off
jostling for position – until the
mountain gradually takes its toll.

Early Sep **Braemar Highland
Gathering**
Braemar, Grampian
Considered by many to be the finest
Highland Gathering of them all, set
amidst the picturesque backdrop of
Deeside. The Queen and the Royal
Family regularly travel up from
neighbouring Balmoral.
The gathering includes all the
traditional events, such as caber-
tossing, sword dancing and pipe
bands – all of the highest calibre.

★Dec 31 **Flambeaux Procession**
Comrie, Tayside
Hogmanay (New Year's Eve) is
celebrated with great fervour
throughout Scotland; but here at
Comrie they have a unique torchlight
procession, accompanied by bagpipes,
which marches through the streets to
the town square. Many of the participants wear outlandish fancy dress,
and there is a general carnival atmosphere. This custom is said to have
originated as an ancient pagan rite.

★Dec 31 **Swinging the Fireballs**
Stonehaven, Grampian
Another unique Hogmanay
celebration, which the locals believe is
derived from a superstition which was
prevalent in the early Middle Ages.
The fire-swingers swing balls of fire
which are made from oil-soaked rags in
wire netting attached to ropes. The
fireball parade proceeds down the
High Street making an eerie sight.
Originally the townspeople believed
that these fireballs would charm the
sun into gradually becoming warmer
through the long cold months of the
winter.

Northern Ireland

Mar 17 **Ballycastle Show**
Ballycastle, Antrim
The Ballycastle and District Annual
Horse Ploughing Match and Heavy
Horse Show is held at Magherintemple
near Fair Head each St Patrick's Day.
The show started late in the 19th c.
and is thought to be the only one in the
world which is held exclusively for
horse-drawn ploughs (no tractors are
allowed). A wide variety of events,
including competitions for ploughmen
and ploughwomen and a 'Style and
Appearance' event showing off these
great horses at their best.

Apr **Feis Dhoire Cholmcille**
Londonderry
Each year a series of Fleadh Cheoils
(festivals of traditional music and
dancing) are held all over Northern
Ireland, with one in each of the six
counties. These usually begin in May,
and each one is composed of a series of
competition heats for the great All-
Ireland finals which take place in
August in the Republic of Ireland. The
events include fiddling, tin-whistling,
singing and traditional dancing – and
everyone attends with the idea of
enjoying themselves. The wildness of
the late-night celebrations has to be
seen to be believed.

4th May **Pipe Band Championships**
Enniskillen, Co Fermanagh
Anyone who believes that bagpipes
and kilted pipe bands are a purely
Scots tradition should go to these
championships. Here pipe bands from
all over the province parade and
compete, giving displays of the highest
order. There are also traditional
entertainments.

Early Jun **Mourne Walk**
Annalong, Co Down
This event, which is promoted by the
Youth Hostels Association of Northern
Ireland, is the province's main hill-
walking event. The 22-mile course
covers the highest peaks of the
beautiful Mountains of Mourne in the

south-eastern corner of Ulster. The entire walk covers ascents totalling over 10,000ft and walkers who complete the course between 7am and 7pm receive a special certificate. This non-competitive event is highly popular and the participants have to be limited to 2000.

Jul 12 Battle of the Boyne Celebrations

Belfast and other towns and villages throughout the province

The 'Twelfth' is Protestant Ulster's big day. This commemorates the Battle of the Boyne, fought in 1690, when William of Orange defeated the Roman Catholic King James II. As a consequence of this the Orange Order (a strictly Protestant organisation) was founded in 1795, and to this day its members are known as 'Orangemen'. On the Twelfth the Orangemen hold big parades with banners and drums, wearing their orange sashes. Afterwards speeches are made on Protestant topics. The biggest parade starts in north Belfast at Carlisle Circus at 10am and is so well attended that it usually takes 2½ hours for the entire procession to leave this point. On the eve of these celebrations bonfires are lit in Protestant areas throughout the province.

Jul 13 The Sham Fight

Scarva, Co Down

The Sham Fight is an historical re-enactment on the theme of the Battle of the Boyne, and the custom dates from the 19th c. This highly popular event often attracts crowds of 25,000 or more, and the main feature is a colourful parade with figures in historical costume on horseback, followed by the ritual 'fight' between two figures dressed as King William III and King James II.

Late Jul Lady of the Lake Festival

Around Irvinestown, Lower Loch Erne, Co Fermanagh

A 12-day festival with a wide range of cultural events and entertainments. These include parades, song contests, children's competitions and many sporting events, especially water sports on the lake. The festival owes its name to a legendary lady who used to make her way through the mists across the lake from island to island. (Her route is still pointed out, and old villagers still believe that her appearance heralds fine weather and good fortune.)

*Late Jul-early Aug Lughnasa Medieval Fair

Carrickfergus, Co Antrim

This ancient fair celebrates the old Celtic quarterly feast of Lughnasa. Originally this feast was associated with the harvest, and was an occasion for games of all kinds. Nowadays the fair is centred on the splendid Norman building of Carrickfergus Castle, where there are medieval entertainments and stalls.

*1st Sun in Aug The Auld Lammas Fair

Shores of Loch Neagh, nr Cookstown, Co Tyrone

An ancient Lammas-tide fair which attracts visitors from all over the province. Stalls are set up selling a wide range of goods, from clothes and bric-à-brac antiques to traditional 'yellowman' confectionery (shaped sweets).

Orangemen's parade

Weekend in early Aug **All-Ireland Road Bowls Final**
Cathedral Road, Armagh City
This ancient game of bowls is known locally as 'bullets', perhaps because the original bowls used were cannon balls. The game is played over a two-mile course along a small curving country road, and the idea is to see who can cover the course in the least amount of throws. This apparently simple game in fact requires a decided amount of skill, and the great heroes of the game are celebrated in traditional ballads. The game is also notorious for betting, and though it has died out over many parts of Ireland it still has a strong following in Co Armagh and Co Cork.

Aug 12 **Relief of Derry Celebrations**
Londonderry
The main feature of these celebrations is the parade of the Apprentice Boys of Derry. This is in fact an adult organisation named after the apprenctices who in 1688 closed the city gates in the face of the army of James II, thus precipitating the 105-day Siege of Derry. The Apprentice Boys lay a wreath at the War Memorial, and then march to St Columb's Cathedral for a thanksgiving service.

Aug 15 **Ancient Order of Hibernians' Processions**
All over Northern Ireland
This is the Roman Catholic Population's answer to the Protestant 'Twelfth' celebrations. It is held on Lady Day and celebrates the long dedication of the people of Ireland to the Roman Catholic church. This custom first started early in this century, and after parades with pipes and bands and church services, Gaelic Games are held. These are attended by members of the Ancient Order of Hibernians in their regalia.

*Last Mon & Tues in Aug **Ould Lammas Fair**
Ballycastle, Co Antrim
This traditional Lammas-tide fair is the main summer fair in the province. Unlike many such fairs, this one still retains much of its practical and commercial nature. There are livestock sales, as well as street stalls selling all kinds of local delicacies, such as dulse (dried edible seaweed) and traditional 'yellowman' confectionery. The fair was established by a charter in 1606, but it had almost certainly been taking place for several centuries before this official recognition.

Sep 23 **Harvest Fair**
Newtonards, Co Down
A seasonal fair which has its origins in the close connection between the people of Scotland and the people of Northern Ireland. It is claimed that two centuries ago this fair was started by Scots traders who sailed the 20 miles across from Scotland early in the morning, set up stalls to sell their wares, and then sailed back in the evening. Now more of a fun fair, the present fair still has stallholders.

1st Sat in Oct **Mounthill Fair**
Mounthill, Co Antrim
This was originally a 17th-c. horse fair, which lapsed with the recession in the horse trade. However, in 1960 the fair was revived, and now has stalls, as well as selling livestock.

2nd & 3rd weeks in Nov **Belfast Festival**
Belfast, Co. Antrim
This is the biggest arts festival in Ireland, and one of the largest in Britain. It features classical and popular music, drama and arts.
See *Festivals*, p. 94

Dec 19 **Closing of the Gates Celebrations**
Londonderry
In 1688 the army of James II approached the gates of Londonderry, and the military governor, Lt-Col Robert Lundy, prepared to surrender. However, when King James's troops were just 60 yards from the gates 13 apprentice boys stole the keys to the city and slammed the gates closed. To commemorate these events the present Apprentice Boys ceremonially burn an effigy of the 'traitor' Lundy.

Useful Addresses & References

Regional Tourist Offices

All these offices welcome personal callers except those marked †(written and telephone enquiries) Most towns also have information centres.

British Tourist Authority
'Welcome to Britain'
Tourist Information Centre
64 St James's Street
London SW1A 1NF
Tel (01) 499 9325

†Cumbria Tourist Board
Ellerthwaite, Windermere
Cumbria LA23 2AQ
Tel (09662) 4444

East Anglia Tourist Board
(Cambridgeshire, Essex, Norfolk & Suffolk)
14 Museum Street, Ipswich
Suffolk IP1 1HU
Tel (0473) 214211

†East Midlands Tourist Board
(Derbyshire, Leicestershire, Lincolnshire, Northamptonshire & Nottinghamshire)
Exchequergate, Lincoln LN2 1PZ
Tel: Lincoln (0522) 31521

†Heart of England Tourist Board
(Gloucester, Hereford & Worcester, Salop, Staffordshire, Warwickshire & West Midlands)
PO Box 15, Worcester WR1 2JT
Tel: Worcester (0905) 29511

London Tourist Board
26 Grosvenor Gardens
London SW1W 0DU
Tel: London (01) 730 0791

Northumbria Tourist Board
(Cleveland, Durham, Northumberland, Tyne & Wear)
9 Osborne Terrace
Newcastle upon Tyne, NE2 1NT
Tel: Newcastle upon Tyne
(0632) 817744

†North West Tourist Board
(Cheshire, Greater Manchester, Lancashire & Merseyside)
The Last Drop Village, Bromley Cross
Bolton BL7 9PZ
Tel: Bolton (0204) 591511

South East England Tourist Board
(Kent, Surrey & Sussex)
Cheviot House, 4-6 Monson Road
Tunbridge Wells, Kent TN1 1NH
Tel: Tunbridge Wells (0892) 40766

Southern Tourist Board
(East Dorset, Hampshire & Isle of Wight)
The Old Town Hall, Leigh Road
Eastleigh, Hampshire SO5 4DE
Tel: Eastleigh (0703) 616027

Thames & Chilterns Tourist Board
(Bedfordshire, Berkshire, Buckingham-shire, Hertfordshire & Oxfordshire)
8 The Market Place, Abingdon
Oxfordshire OX14 3UD
Tel: Abingdon (0235) 22711

West Country Tourist Board
(Avon, Cornwall, Devon, West Dorset, Somerset, Wiltshire & Isles of Scilly)
Trinity Court, 37 Southernhay East
Exeter, Devon EX1 1QS
Tel: Exeter (0392) 76351

Yorkshire and Humberside Tourist Board
(Humberside, North, South & West Yorkshire)
312 Tadcaster Road, York YO2 2HP
Tel: York (0904) 707961

Isle of Man Tourist Board
13 Victoria Street, Douglas
Isle of Man
Tel: Douglas (0624) 4323

Isle of Wight Tourist Board
21 High Street, Newport
Isle of Wight PO30 1JS
Tel: Newport (0983) 524343 or 525141

Scottish Tourist Board
23 Ravelston Terrace, Edinburgh
EH4 3EU
Tel: Edinburgh (031) 332 2433

Wales Tourist Board
3 Castle Street, Cardiff CF1 2RE
Tel: Cardiff (0222) 27281

Northern Ireland Tourist Board
River House, 48 High Street
Belfast BT1 2DS
Tel: Belfast (0232) 31221 or 46609

Festivals

Aldeburgh Festival
High Street, Aldeburgh
Suffolk IP15 5AX
Tel: Aldeburgh (072 885) 2935

Bath Festival
Linley House
1 Pierrepoint Place, Bath BA1 1JY
Tel: Bath (0225) 62231

Belfast Festival
8 Malone Road, Belfast BT9 5BN
Tel: Belfast (0232) 667687

Cheltenham Festival
Town Hall, Cheltenham
Gloucestershire GL50 1QA
Tel: Cheltenham (0242) 21621

Chichester Festivities
Canon Gate House, South Street
Chichester, Sussex PO19 1PU
Tel: Chichester (0243) 785718

City of London Festival
64 West Smithfield,
London EC1A 9DY
Tel: London (01) 606 1973

Edinburgh International Festival
21 Market Street, Edinburgh
Edinburgh EH1 1BW
Tel: Edinburgh (031) 226 4001

Glyndebourne Festival Opera
Glyndebourne, near Lewes
East Sussex BN8 5UU
Tel: Ringmer (0273) 812321

Harrogate Festival
Royal Baths, Harrogate
North Yorkshire HG21 2RR
Tel: Harrogate (0423) 62303

International Musical Eisteddfod
The Armoury, Llangollen
Clwyd LL20 8NG
Tel: Llangollen (0978) 860236

Three Choirs Festival
20 Walney Lane, Hereford
Tel: Hereford (0432) 6461

References for traditional recipes

Elisabeth Ayrton *The Cookery of England* (André Deutsch, 1975)

Mrs Beeton *The Book of Household Management* (Ward, Lock & Tyler, 1859)

Lizzie Boyd (Ed.), *British Cookery*, (Croom Helm, 1976)

Elizabeth Craig *The Scottish Cookery Book* (André Deutsch, 1965)

Elizabeth David *English Bread and Yeast Cookery* (Penguin, 1979)

Elizabeth David *Spices, Salt and Aromatics in the English Kitchen* (Penguin, 1970)

Jane Grigson *English Food* (Penguin, 1977)

David Mabey *In Search of Food* (Macdonald & Jane's, 1978)

Michael Smith, *Fine English Cookery* (Faber, 1977)

The W. I. Diamond Jubilee Cookbook (Pan 1977)

Look out for booklets of regional recipes, often privately published and sold in museums and craft shops. The following publications are available from tourist information centres: *A Guide to English Food & Drink and Where to Enjoy It; A Taste of Scotland; A Taste of Wales; Dining in Ireland.*

Trusthouse Forte Central Reservations Office
For world-wide reservations at any THF Hotel telephone (01) 567 3444

Index

*Page numbers in
italics indicate
illustrations*